D1528231

E A S T E R

Meditations for Addicts

Mark E. Shaw &
Shirley Crowder

EASTER: Meditations for Addicts
© 2022 Mark E. Shaw & Shirley Crowder

ISBN: 9798408580613

All rights reserved. No part of this publication may be reproduced or transmitted in any form or by any means without written permission from the publisher.

Unless otherwise noted all Scripture quotations have been taken from the *Christian Standard Bible*®, Copyright © 2017 by Holman Bible Publishers. Used by permission. Christian Standard Bible® and CSB® are federally registered trademarks of Holman Bible Publishers.

Scriptures marked "ESV" are from *The Holy Bible*, English Standard Version®, copyright © 2001 by Crossway, 2011 Text Edition. Used by permission. All rights reserved.

Scriptures marked "NIV" are from *The Holy Bible, New International Version*®, copyright © 1973, 1978, 1984, 2011 by Biblical, Inc.™ Used by permission of Zondervan. All rights reserved worldwide. www.zondervan.com.

Scriptures marked "NKJV" are from *The Holy Bible, New King James Version*®, copyright © 1982 by Thomas Nelson Publishers, Nashville. Used by permission. All rights reserved.

Scripture passages may be found at BlueLetterBible.org.

All hymn lyrics are Public Domain and are from HymnTime.com.

Cover cross: https://www.canstockphoto.com/red-cross-on-black-background-14682455.html

Chapter Title Page Illustrations: See "Chapter Title Page Illustrations Credits" on page 248.

THE ADDICTION CONNECTION
10 Years

The Addiction Connection
9379 Gunpowder Road
Florence KY 41042
www.theaddictionconnection.org

Dedication

We dedicate this book to those

struggling with an addiction.

As you work through these meditations,

may these biblical truths point you to Jesus —

the only source of Hope and help

that comes through a strengthened

relationship with Jesus Christ.

All Scripture is inspired by God
and is profitable for teaching,
for rebuking, for correcting,
for training in righteousness,
so that the man of God may be complete,
equipped for every good work.
2 Timothy 3:16-17

Table of Contents

Acknowledgments

We are grateful the Lord allowed us to collaborate on this meditative journey through the Easter season for those struggling with addiction.

The Lord has been gracious to allow us to minister alongside each other for many years. Serving in ministry together over the years continues to be a blessing, and we look forward to serving together in the time the Lord allows us in the future.

We are humbled and grateful for the countless sisters and brothers in Christ who have prayed for us and encouraged us in our ministries and as we wrote these Easter meditations.

We are thankful for the guidance, support, encouragement, and prayers of Mary Shaw (Mark's wife), LaVerne Marshall (Shirley's high school English teacher), and Baker Hill (Shirley's Nigeria MK cousin) who helped us refine this manuscript.

About the Cover

Look at the cover. The black represents the darkness and chaos of addiction (all sin, actually). The red cross breaks through the blackness to represent the shed blood of Christ breaking through the blackness of our sin.

During the Easter season, we celebrate the death, burial, and resurrection of Jesus Christ, the Messiah. Through the shedding of His blood on the cross, He atoned[1] for our sins. When we come to Him in faith, asking, He forgives us.

> *For God was pleased to have all his fullness dwell in him, and through him to reconcile everything to himself, whether things on earth or things in heaven, by making peace, through his blood, shed on the cross* (Colossians 1:19-20).

---

[1] Reconciliation of God to man through the shed blood of Jesus on the cross.

Meditations for Addicts Series

The *Meditations for Addicts* Series is comprised of meditations for those struggling or suffering with addiction. Everyone, not only those with an addictive habit, needs as much biblically-oriented help as we can obtain to facilitate our being more and more transformed into the image of Christ.

It is important to note that when we use the term "addict" that we are not categorizing or demeaning any person struggling or suffering with an addiction. Instead, we use the term because it is the term that most people in society know.

As you work through these meditations and the Interaction Exercises for each day, we pray the Holy Spirit will stir your soul to love and good deeds as He helps you embrace the Savior as never before. The series includes not only the holiday seasons that those struggling or suffering with an addiction may find difficult, but other topics to encourage them in their daily walk with Christ.

Introduction

What emotional reaction do you have when you think of Easter? Do you remember joyous celebrations with your family and friends? Maybe you fondly remember an Easter outfit you wore to Easter Sunday services at church. Did your family gather for an Easter feast? Or is the opposite true? Does the thought of Easter make you anxious? Do you dread the obligatory church attendance and family celebration? Maybe you just want to hide until it is all over!

Many people—not just those struggling with addictive habits—have a difficult time during the Easter season. Painful memories of family and friends who are no longer living, missed opportunities, or broken relationships can plague you during a time designed for celebration. Regret can often fill your mind, too, as you remember hurtful things you said and have done. Regret can also fill your mind because of what you failed to say or do in the past.

Holidays can also be difficult for the person struggling with an addiction who is learning to trust in God and His provision, to put away addictive desires and behaviors, and put on godly thoughts, attitudes, and behaviors.

It is ironic that while you celebrate the finished work of Jesus Christ on the cross and your new life in Him, you often become so busy with all the church activities that you forget to spend time thanking, praising, and meditating upon Him and His sacrifice.

For this reason, our book is intended to help you to begin your Easter celebration early so you can focus your heart and reflect upon the events leading up to the death, burial, and resurrection of Jesus Christ from the dead.

Easter is a time to remember that God sent His only begotten Son, Jesus, to earth to live as fully God and fully man. Jesus' mission was to live a perfect life so that He could pay the price to purchase and save you from the penalty of your sins. Addiction is the result of sinful heart desires fulfilled in choices that render a person helpless and enslaved to something dangerous, but God wants so much more for you than enslavement to substances or pleasures that only harm.

For this reason, God sent His Son, Jesus, to live a sinless life on earth so that by His sacrifice, He provided you with an opportunity to be saved and later sanctified. Jesus took upon Himself not only your sin, but also the punishment and wrath of God that you, and all of us, deserve. That sacrifice fulfilled God's promise to save sinful women and men who repent[2] and place their faith in Christ alone for eternal life. Therefore, the Easter season is a gift to all believers, as well as a call for you to share the only message of Hope available to sinful man, which includes those whom the world calls the addicted.

By God's grace, you are able to receive that precious gift of salvation and experience God through the indwelling of His Holy Spirit. Salvation is not just temporal (for this life), it is eternal (for life everlasting). Only God can give such a precious gift!

The Purpose of These Meditations

During the weeks leading up to Easter you can ensure your relationship with God stays strong by guarding your time with Him and keeping Christ as the focus of your Easter celebrations. It is, of course, the attitude of your heart when you approach God that makes the difference in how you experience Easter.

If you view your Easter preparation and celebration as a means of enabling you — a Christ-follower — to draw closer to your Savior and Lord Jesus, you will enjoy knowing

---

[2] Turning to God and turning away from your sin. –Dr. Howard A. Eyrich

Him better as these practices help connect you with Christ and His Word in a more intimate manner. The Easter season is for you, even if you have struggled, or are still struggling, with addictive choices, since addiction primarily stems from a sin issue of the heart for which Jesus Christ died. Viewing addiction biblically is key for setting you free.

If there is unconfessed sin in your heart, there could likely be a barrier between you and God, and your worship of Him will be hindered. Therefore, when the Holy Spirit convicts[3] you of sin in your heart, be quick to confess[4] and repent of that sin, ask God to forgive[5] you, and walk in the freedom of that forgiveness. Then, worship God freely and without restraint, resting in the finished work of Jesus Christ and His resurrection. Easter serves as a reminder to do just that!

As the authors of these meditations, we pray you will recognize the incredible gift of salvation God has provided

---

[3] When the Holy Spirit files charges against you that what you thought, said, or did was sinful (violated God's law). As a result, you experience guilt over your sin. –Dr. Howard A. Eyrich

[4] Admitting to God that you sinned. It is a statement of your admission of guilt, without excuse. This statement of ownership gives the Judge (God) the opportunity to grant forgiveness (1 John 1:9). –Dr. Howard A. Eyrich

[5] When God chooses to forget your sin and not hold you accountable for it. Your sin is buried in the deepest sea (Micah 7:19). –Dr. Howard A. Eyrich

for every repentant person, including those struggling with addictive choices who sometimes mistakenly think they are wicked sinners beyond God's reach. But nothing could be further from the truth! We believe the Lord will be pleased to use this meditative journey to prepare you to celebrate Easter as you keep your heart and mind focused on Him in the weeks leading up to Easter. We hope that your heart will be transformed by the truth of who Jesus is, what He has done for you in the past, what He is doing for you in the present, and what He will do for you in the future.

Fully God and Fully Man

Begin Five Sundays Before Easter

Celebrate Easter This Week

Begin each day by confessing your sin and asking God to forgive your sin.

Pray your heart will be open to the correction, encouragement, and teaching of God's Word.

Pray the Lord will ignite your passion to know Him better and to share about His sacrificial gift, Jesus, with all those whom He brings across your path.

Take your time as you work through each day's reading to consider prayerfully and write out your answers to the exercises.

Day 1

Old Testament Prophecy[6]

For a child will be born for us, a son will be given to us, and the government will be on his shoulders. He will be named Wonderful Counselor, Mighty God, Eternal Father, Prince of Peace (Isaiah 9:6).

---

[6] God gave prophets knowledge to declare what would happen in the future.

✞ To which of these names of Jesus (Wonderful Counselor, Mighty God, Eternal Father, Prince of Peace) are you most drawn? Explain why?

New Testament Fulfillment[7]

¹In the beginning was the Word, and the Word was with God, and the Word was God. ²He was with God in the beginning ... ¹⁴The Word became flesh and dwelt among us. We observed his glory, the glory as the one and only Son from the Father, full of grace and truth (John 1:1-2, 14).

✞ Explain how the fact that God is *full of grace and truth* encourages you in your walk with Christ.

---

[7] When God's prophecies come true.

Symbol of Easter

Turn back to the chapter title page (p 19) and look at the illustration of the shadow of the cross falling across the manger. Since these meditations are supposed to be about Easter, not Christmas, then why are we instructing you to look at a manger? The answer is in Isaiah 9:6, which is the Day 1 Old Testament Prophecy, because it gives you a hint about the importance of the manger in the Easter account. In the first part of the verse, you learn that Jesus is fully man (*a child will be born*) and fully God (*a son will be given*). This concept is called the hypostatic union, a fancy name for the combination of divine and human attributes in the person of Christ. It is impossible for us to understand completely but that does not make it untrue! It is true and only God understands it completely as He uses this concept to bridge the gap between mankind and Himself.

The shadow of the cross on the manger is a poignant and sobering reminder as it portrays two essential pieces of the gospel message and the Easter account. The manger reminds us of the gift God gave us—Jesus—God's gift of mercy, grace, and love. Jesus came to earth exactly like the Old Testament prophets foretold that He would.

Unfortunately, some want to focus only upon the deity of Christ without acknowledging His humanity. Yet the manger represents the "fully man" aspect of Jesus. Sadly, many people want to keep Jesus as a cute little baby in the manger by focusing only upon His humanity without recognizing His deity. Jesus is so much more! He is the long-awaited Messiah—our Savior and Lord—fully God and fully man.

Notice how the shadow of the cross on the manger gives you a glimpse of God's plan for Jesus. After outgrowing the manger, we know that *Jesus increased in wisdom and stature, and in favor with God and with people* (Luke 2:52). Jesus walked on this earth teaching, healing the sick, and performing other miracles. Anyone who came in contact with Jesus was changed by their encounter with Him. He walked the earth as both God and man.

God's plan of redemption would be accomplished when Jesus Messiah, the baby in the manger, grew into manhood. Mankind needed to be redeemed (saved) because Adam and Eve sinned against holy God (Genesis 3). God demanded that a *sinless* man pay the price for the sin of all mankind. No person who has ever lived except Jesus has lived perfectly and without sin. Because Jesus is the only human being to live a sinless life since Adam and Eve chose to sin, He alone could pay the price for the sin of mankind. On the cross, Jesus suffered and died the death you deserved. He was then buried and rose from the grave--from death to life—three days later. The finished work of Christ on the cross signified that God's people were not required to repeatedly offer bulls and goats (Hebrews 10:1-18) as sacrifices for their sins as was the old covenant, Jewish custom.

Did you notice in the chapter title page illustration that Jesus is *not* still on the cross? The cross casts its shadow onto the manger without the Person of Jesus still nailed to it. Why? Because after Jesus died on the cross, His dead body was taken down and buried in a borrowed tomb. Then three days later, He arose victorious over death and the grave. The shadow of the cross on the manger reminds us that Jesus came to earth as a baby, lived among us as fully God and fully man, and then faced the violent death of crucifixion before His resurrection took place. God raised Jesus from death to life for His own glory and now Jesus Christ is seated at the right hand of the Father in heaven.

✟ When you first looked at the illustration of the shadow of the cross falling upon the manger, what emotions and thoughts did it evoke? Describe them.

✟ Earlier you read, "Anyone who came in contact with Jesus was changed by that encounter." If you have had an encounter with Jesus, how were you changed as a result of that encounter? If you have not had an encounter with Jesus, read through "Do You Know the Jesus About Whom You Have Been Reading?" on page 235. Also talk with a trusted Christian friend[8] who can help you understand how to come to a saving knowledge of Jesus.

---

[8] Someone you can be completely honest with about everything.

Hymn of Easter

I Cannot Tell is a beautiful hymn written by William Young Fullerton.[9] It is sung to the tune of *Londonderry Air*[10] (*Oh Danny Boy*). We usually hear this hymn at Christmas although its message is for any time of the year.

In the foundational Scripture for this hymn, we know Christ *emptied himself by assuming the form of a servant, taking on the likeness of humanity* (Philippians 2:7).

Notice that each verse begins with the phrase "I cannot tell," acknowledging that since we cannot fully understand God's ways, we do not know how to convey adequately who He is and how He works. It also expresses our amazement that God loved us so much that He sent His Son to earth as a humble servant to save those who believe in Him (John 3:16; Philippians 2:5-11[11]).

As we reach the middle of each stanza, we sing "But this I know." This phrase is our bold proclamation of what we know and understand, through faith.

---

[9] See "Who Was William Young Fullerton?" on p 41.
[10] See "Who Composed the Tune *Londonderry Air*?" on p 42.
[11] See "Supplemental Scripture Reading: Philippians 2:5-11" on p 38.

As we are *being rooted and firmly established in love*, we are able *to comprehend with all the saints what is the length and width, height and depth of God's love* (Ephesians 3:17-18).

Join us in singing.

Stanza 1

I cannot tell why He whom angels worship,

Should set His love upon the sons of men,

Or why, as shepherd, He should seek the wanderers,

To bring them back, they know not how or when.

But this I know, that He was born of Mary

When Bethlehem's manger was His only home,

And that He lived at Nazareth and labored,

And so the Savior, Savior of the world is come.

Stanza 2

I cannot tell how silently He suffered,

As with His peace He graced this place of tears,

Or how His heart upon the cross was broken,

The crown of pain to three and thirty years.

But this I know, He heals the brokenhearted,

And stays our sin, and calms our lurking fear,

And lifts the burden from the heavy laden,

For yet the Savior, Savior of the world is here.

Stanza 3

I cannot tell how He will win the nations,

How He will claim His earthly heritage,

How satisfy the needs and aspirations

Of East and West, of sinner and of sage.

But this I know, all flesh shall see His glory,

And He shall reap the harvest He has sown,

And some glad day His sun shall shine in splendor

When He the Savior, Savior of the world is known.

Stanza 4

I cannot tell how all the lands shall worship,

When, at His bidding, every storm is stilled,

Or who can say how great the jubilation

When all the hearts of men with love are filled.

But this I know, the skies will thrill with rapture,

And myriad, myriad human voices sing,

And earth to Heaven,

And Heaven to earth, will answer:

At last the Savior, Savior of the world is king!

✟ Which of the "I cannot tell" statements in this hymn best expresses the things you do not fully understand about God's ways?

Explain your answer.

✟ Which of the "But this I know" statements gives you the most comfort and strength as you face each day? Explain.

Implications of Fully God and Fully Man for Addicts

The addicted lifestyle is not easy for a number of reasons. Just one of them is the overwhelming feeling of loneliness. Even though others might be using drugs or alcohol right next to you, each person struggling with addictive habits is truly an island to himself. True intimacy, love, and giving friendships appear to be there, but in reality they are lacking. It is a façade. All who use are taking care of themselves first and this lack of real friendship only adds to their loneliness. Immersed in addiction, you think that your non-using buddies do not understand you. It seems like no one really knows you or cares for you. Loneliness is a feeling with which you have become well acquainted.

But in Christ Jesus, you have a Friend who knows what it is like to be human. While Jesus never smoked marijuana or injected a needle into His arm, He knows what it is like to deal with the heart of temptation (Matthew 4:1-11[12]; Luke 4:1-13[13]). Those temptations He experienced as recorded in the sufficient and accurate Word of God contain the basic elements of all temptations. Hebrews 2:17-18 says it best: *Therefore, he had to be like his brothers and sisters in every way, so that he could become a merciful and faithful high priest in matters pertaining to God, to make atonement for the sins of the people. For since he himself has suffered when he was tempted, he is able to help those who are tempted.*

Jesus was truly a complete human being while also being completely God. Jesus being 100% God and 100% man

[12] See "Supplemental Scripture Reading: Matthew 4:1-11" on p 39.
[13] See "Supplemental Scripture Reading: Luke 4:1-13" on p 40.

might blow your mind, but it is a logical, understandable concept even though you do not know all of the details of how it works. No human does. It is a supra-logical[14] concept that the Bible teaches meaning only God can really understand it completely. It is not illogical at all—just supra-logical.

Jesus never sinned in His thoughts, words, or actions. Yet as a human, He knows what it is like to live in the human condition and to be tempted. Being a born-again child of God means you have a Friend who knows what you are going through because He has been there. But better than that, you have a Savior who washes away your sins and provides the indwelling of the Holy Spirit to change your heart desires from selfish ones to godly ones. You never have to walk alone ever again.

Loneliness was a pre-Fall[15] condition (Genesis 2:18) and God said it was *"not good for the man to be alone."* You need Christ and other believers in your life. You cannot isolate for long and stay sober. Loneliness makes battling temptations to sin feel powerful and overwhelming, but

---

[14] This term is not in our dictionary. It is a term Mark first heard from Pastor Harry Reeder at Briarwood PCA in Birmingham, AL. He took the prefix (*supra* which means transcending) and connected it to "logical."
[15] Before Adam and Eve listened to the serpent and disobeyed God by eating of the fruit of the Tree of Life (see Genesis 3).

that is not true. Jesus provided a blueprint for how to deal with any temptation by being led by the power of the Holy Spirit and practically applying the Word of God. Anyone struggling with an addiction can deny the flesh and follow the model that Jesus provides in Matthew 4 and Luke 4, knowing that Jesus is walking with you.

✞ You read that one of the reasons the addicted lifestyle is not easy is because of the overwhelming feelings of loneliness.
Describe a time in your life when you experienced overwhelming feelings of loneliness.

✞ You read "you have a Savior who washes away your sins and provides the indwelling of the Holy Spirit to change your heart desires from selfish ones to godly ones." List your heart desires that you need the Holy Spirit to change into godly ones.

Hymn of Response

How do we respond to God's precious love gift of Jesus Christ, the Messiah, and His finished work on the cross? We sing Joseph Proud's[16] hymn *Great God, We Give Thee Praise*, which is sung to the tune *St. Thomas!*[17] that was composed by Aaron Williams.

Psalm 95:1-6 is a foundational Scripture passage for this hymn as it bids us:

> [1]*Come, let us shout joyfully to the Lord, shout triumphantly to the rock of our salvation!* [2]*Let us enter his presence with thanksgiving; let us shout triumphantly to him in song.* [3]*For the Lord is a great God, a great King above all gods.* [4]*The depths of the earth are in his hand, and the mountain peaks are his.* [5]*The sea is his; he made it. His hands formed the dry land.* [6]*Come, let us worship and bow down; let us kneel before the Lord our Maker.*

Join us in singing to the Lord.

---

[16] See "Who Was Joseph Proud?" on p 43.
[17] See "Who Composed the Tune *St Thomas*?" on p 44.

Stanza 1

Great God, we give Thee praise

For all Thy wondrous grace

Thy wise and ever loving ways

To all our favored race.

We hear and talk so much about God's grace that it sometimes becomes commonplace for us, and we forget how wondrous it really is. *For* [we] *are saved by grace through faith, and this is not from* [ourselves]; *it is God's gift* (Ephesians 2:8) to those He *has chosen … to be his own possession* (Deuteronomy 14:2). Now that is a reason to praise God!

Stanza 2

Thou hast Thy love revealed

Beyond what prophets knew;

Thy holy Book of truth unsealed

To our astonished view.

I love the picture in this stanza of God revealing more about Himself through the Bible that the prophets did not know, as Hebrews 1:1-3 tells us.

[1]Long ago God spoke to the fathers by the prophets at different times in different ways. [2]In these last days, he has spoken to us by his Son. God has

appointed him heir of all things and made the universe through Him. ³The Son is the radiance of God's glory and the exact expression of his nature, sustaining all things by his powerful word. ³After making purification for sins, he sat down at the right hand of the Majesty on high.

Jesus perfectly revealed God in and through everything that He taught and did.

Stanza 3
We wander now no more
Where darkening errors lead,
But truth by light divine explore,
And wonder while we read.

We could quit wandering in the darkness when *the Word became flesh and dwelt among us* (John 1:14). Jesus is *the way, the truth, and the life* that leads us to our Heavenly Father (John 14:6).

Referring to Jesus as the Word reminds us that Jesus was fully God and fully man, who lived and walked on earth.

Stanza 4
Lord, we adore Thy name
For light and truth divine!

From Thee the welcomed mercies came,

And be the glory Thine.

Oh, how welcomed God's mercy is! Someone defined mercy as not getting what we deserve. God sent Jesus to the world to save sinners—which all of us are. We give thanks to the Lord who is *full of compassion, and gracious, longsuffering and abundant in mercy and truth* (Psalm 86:15 NKJV).

✣ In the third stanza, we sing about how we could quit wandering in the darkness when *the Word became flesh and dwelt among us* (John 1:14). as fully God and fully man. Describe ways you have quit wandering in the darkness.

If you have not quit wandering in the darkness or uncertain what it means to wander in the darkness, read "Do You Know the Jesus About Whom You Have Been Reading?" on page 235. Also talk with a trusted Christian friend who can help you understand how to quit wandering in the darkness.

✞ Mercy is not getting what we deserve. Explain how you have experienced God's mercy in your life.

Prayer

Gracious Heavenly Father, thank You for the manger that held baby Jesus—Your gift of mercy, grace, and love to us. Thank You that He lived on earth as fully God and fully man so that we could be saved. In Jesus' Name, Amen.

Remember Jesus was Fully God and Fully Man

"A man who was merely a man and said the sort of things Jesus said would not be a great moral teacher. He would either be a lunatic—on the level with the man who says he is a poached egg—or else he would be the Devil of Hell. You must make your choice. Either this man was, and is, the Son of God; or else a madman or something worse."
– C. S. Lewis, *Mere Christianity*

Prayers, Notes, & Questions

NOTE: If you need more room, see page 239.

Supplemental Scripture Reading

Philippians 2:5-11

[5]Adopt the same attitude as that of Christ Jesus, [6]who, existing in the form of God, did not consider equality with God as something to be exploited. [7]Instead he emptied himself by assuming the form of a servant, taking on the likeness of humanity. And when he had come as a man, [8]he humbled himself by becoming obedient to the point of death—even to death on a cross.

[9]For this reason God highly exalted him and gave him the name that is above every name, [10]so that at the name of Jesus every knee will bow—in heaven and on earth and under the earth—[11]and every tongue will confess that Jesus Christ is Lord, to the glory of God the Father.

Supplemental Scripture Reading

Matthew 4:1-11

¹*Then Jesus was led up by the Spirit into the wilderness to be tempted by the devil.* ²*After he had fasted forty days and forty nights, he was hungry.* ³*Then the tempter approached him and said, "If you are the Son of God, tell these stones to become bread."* ⁴*He answered, "It is written: Man must not live on bread alone but on every word that comes from the mouth of God."*

⁵*Then the devil took him to the holy city, had him stand on the pinnacle of the temple,* ⁶*and said to him, "If you are the Son of God, throw yourself down. For it is written: He will give his angels orders concerning you, and they will support you with their hands so that you will not strike your foot against a stone."* ⁷*Jesus told him, "It is also written: Do not test the Lord your God."* ⁸*Again, the devil took him to a very high mountain and showed him all the kingdoms of the world and their splendor.* ⁹*And he said to him, "I will give you all these things if you will fall down and worship me."* ¹⁰*Then Jesus told him, "Go away, Satan! For it is written: Worship the Lord your God, and serve only him."* ¹¹*Then the devil left him, and angels came and began to serve him.*

Supplemental Scripture Reading

Luke 4:1-13

¹Then Jesus left the Jordan, full of the Holy Spirit, and was led by the Spirit in the wilderness ²For forty days to be tempted by the devil. He ate nothing during those days, and when they were over, he was hungry. ³The devil said to him, "If you are the Son of God, tell this stone to become bread." ⁴But Jesus answered him, "It is written: Man must not live on bread alone."

⁵So he took him up and showed him all the kingdoms of the world in a moment of time. ⁶The devil said to him, "I will give you their splendor and all this authority, because it has been given over to me, and I can give it to anyone I want. ⁷"If you, then, will worship me, all will be yours." ⁸And Jesus answered him, "It is written: Worship the Lord your God, and serve him only."

⁹So he took him to Jerusalem, had him stand on the pinnacle of the temple, and said to him, "If you are the Son of God, throw yourself down from here. ¹⁰"For it is written: He will give his angels orders concerning you, to protect you, ¹¹they will support you with their hands, so that you will not strike your foot against a stone." ¹²And Jesus answered him, "It is said: Do not test the Lord your God." ¹³After the devil had finished every temptation, he departed from him for a time.

Who Was William Young Fullerton?

William Young Fullerton[18] lived in the United Kingdom from 1857 to 1932. He was a Baptist preacher and writer who was influenced by the preaching of Charles Haddon Spurgeon, whom he considered a mentor and friend.

Fullerton compiled numerous hymnals. He wrote biographies of John Bunyan, Charles Haddon Spurgeon, James William Condell Fegan, and Frederick Brotherton Meyer. He also wrote missionary histories and devotionals.

I Cannot Tell is the only hymn Fullerton is known to have written.

---

[18] https://bit.ly/WYFullerton

Who Composed the Tune
Londonderry Air?

According to legend, Miss Jane Ross, who lived in Limavady, Ireland, was the first to notate[19] an air[20] she heard an itinerant fiddler playing in 1851. Tradition names a blind man from Myroe, Ireland, Jimmy McCurry, as the tune's fiddler. He regularly attended and played at the weekly market opposite her house.

The tune we now know as *Londonderry Air*, is perhaps one of the world's best-known melodies. It was published in the 1855 book *The Ancient Music of Ireland*, in which it was listed as an anonymous air attributing Jane Ross as the collector.

Its title is descriptive, referring to Londonderry County, where it was collected.[21]

---

[19] Using symbols to write music on musical staff paper.
[20] Likely a translation of the word *aria*, an Italian term. It is melody in choral music.
[21] BBC Radio: Your Place and Mine - https://bbc.in/2YJOn8V and Wilifried F. Voss - https://bit.ly/3ndz55R

Who Was Joseph Proud?

Joseph Proud[22] lived from 1745 to 1826. He was an English Swedenborgian minister who was a gifted preacher. He authored numerous publications. His hymns are still used in Swedenborgian worship.

In addition to *Great God, We Give Thee Praise*, he also wrote the powerful hymn, *Down From the Worlds of Radiant Light*, and many other hymns.

---

[22] https://bit.ly/JosephProud

Who Composed the Tune
St. Thomas?

Aaron Williams[23] lived in London, England, from 1731 to 1776. He composed the tune *St. Thomas*, to which *Great God, We Give You Praise* is sung.

Williams was a music engraver and clerk at the Scottish Church, London Wall. He published several church music collections, as well as numerous tunes that are the basis for many hymns.

In addition to the tune *St. Thomas*, Williams also composed the tune *Dover*, to which the hymn *O God, My Heavenly King* is sung.

---

[23] https://bit.ly/Aaron-Williams

The Triumphal Entry

Begin Four Sundays Before Easter

Celebrate Easter This Week

Begin each day by confessing your sin and asking God to forgive your sin.

Pray your heart will be open to the correction, encouragement, and teaching of God's Word.

Pray the Lord will ignite your passion to know Him better and to celebrate and worship Jesus in the same manner He was worshiped during His triumphal entry.

Take your time as you work through each day's reading to consider prayerfully and write out your answers to the exercises.

DAY 1

Old Testament Prophecy

Rejoice greatly, Daughter Zion![24] Shout in triumph, Daughter Jerusalem! Look, your King is coming to you; he is righteous and victorious, humble and riding on a donkey, on a colt, the foal of a donkey (Zechariah 9:9).

---

[24] A title for Jerusalem, God's holy city.

✟ To which of these facts (righteous, victorious, humble) about King Jesus are you most drawn? Explain why.

New Testament Fulfillment

¹When they approached Jerusalem and came to Bethphage at the Mount of Olives, Jesus then sent two disciples, ²telling them, "Go into the village ahead of you. At once you will find a donkey tied there with her foal. Untie them and bring them to me. ³If anyone says anything to you, say that the Lord needs them, and he will send them at once." ⁴This took place so that what was spoken through the prophet might be fulfilled: ⁵Tell Daughter Zion, "See, your King is coming to you, gentle, and mounted on a donkey, and on a colt, the foal of a donkey." ⁶The disciples went and did just as Jesus directed them (Matthew 21:1-6).

✟ In this passage, Jesus tells His disciples to go do something out of the ordinary, and they went and did what Jesus told them to do without asking any questions or expressing any doubts about doing what He asked. Describe a time in your life when God has led you to do something through His Holy Spirit-inspired Word, and you either obeyed without question or doubt, or questioned and doubted instead of obeying.

DAY 2

Symbol of Easter

Turn back to the chapter title page (p 45) and look at the illustration of the palm branches and the donkey—two symbols of Easter that are important elements of Jesus' triumphal entry into Jerusalem.

As our Day 1 Old Testament Prophecy told us and our New Testament Fulfillment described, Jesus rode triumphantly into Jerusalem on a donkey while the people laid their cloaks and palm branches on the ground, waved palm branches in the air, and shouted "Hosanna!"[25]

---

[25] Means "Save, we pray!" –Smith Bible Dictionary

Jesus' triumphal entry into Jerusalem is celebrated today as Palm Sunday. John's account tells us:

> *12The next day, when the large crowd that had come to the festival heard that Jesus was coming to Jerusalem, 13they took palm branches and went out to meet him. They kept shouting:* **"Hosanna! Blessed is he who comes in the name of the Lord—the King of Israel!"** (John 12:12-13)

The palm branches are date palms, very tall trees that grow well and thrive in the Holy Land. Their long, large leaves were perfect for padding the way of the donkey as well as for waving in the air as the people welcomed and praised God.

In ancient times, palm branches symbolized goodness, well-being, grandeur, steadfastness, and victory. They were often depicted on coins and important buildings. King Solomon *carved all the surrounding temple walls with carved engravings—cherubim, palm trees, and flower blossoms—in the inner and outer sanctuaries* (1 Kings 6:29).

Palm branches were regarded as tokens of joy and triumph and were customarily used on festive occasions (Leviticus 23:40, Nehemiah 8:15). Kings and conquerors were welcomed with palm branches being strewn before them and waved in the air. Victors of Grecian games returned to their homes triumphantly waving palm branches in their hands. We read in Revelation 7:9 that an innumerable multitude of people from *every nation, tribe, people, and language,* are going to stand before Jesus, with palm branches in their hands, honoring Him when He returns.[26]

"Clip, clop, clop. Clip, clop, clop." These were the words sung in a children's Christmas program. The children were, of course, singing about the donkey that Mary may have ridden when she and Joseph were heading to Bethlehem to be registered for the census, and more importantly, for the birth of Jesus Christ, the Messiah.

Today we are looking at another donkey, the one that Jesus rode as He made His triumphal entry into Jerusalem that eventually led to His death. The "clip, clop, clop" of this donkey was softened by the palm branches and clothing laid on the ground. And, of course, the "clip, clop, clop" could not be heard over the loud "Hosannas!" being shouted by the crowd.

The donkey is known as a beast of burden that is accustomed to carrying loads from one place to another.

---

[26] See "Supplemental Scripture: Matthew 21:7-17" on p 69.

On this day, she was simply doing what she was created to do, carry loads from one place to another. A preacher once said, this donkey was simply doing what she always did, something that was normally viewed as commonplace and insignificant, carrying a load or person. In the process, she did something extraordinarily significant—carrying Jesus Christ, the Messiah, into Jerusalem.

Instead of coming in on a warhorse ready to do battle, Jesus coming into Jerusalem on a donkey showed that He was coming not only in peace, but also to bring peace.

In this exciting event, King Jesus was not riding into Jerusalem to establish an earthly kingdom; He was riding into Jerusalem to be accused falsely, beaten, and crucified on the cross until He died.

✞ We read that "an innumerable multitude of people from *every nation, tribe, people, and language*, are going to stand before Jesus, with palm branches in their hands, honoring Him when He returns." Are you going to be among that multitude of people (Christ-followers)? If you know you will not be, or you are not certain if you will be, take some time to consider prayerfully "Do You Know the Jesus About Whom You Have Been

Reading?" on page 235. Talk with a trusted Christian friend who can help you understand how to come to a saving knowledge of Jesus.

✝ The donkey that carried Jesus into Jerusalem "was simply doing what she was created to do," and "in the process, she did something extraordinary and very significant." What ordinary things that you do can be used by God as something extraordinary?

DAY 3

Hymn of Easter

Do you know the wonderful hymn *Ride on, Ride on In Majesty!* for which Henry Hart Milman[27] wrote the lyrics

---

[27] See "Who Was Henry Hart Milman?" on p 74.

that are sung to the tune *Hebron*,[28] composed by Lowell Mason? The hymn is based on the Day 1 Old Testament Prophecy (p 46) and its New Testament Fulfillment (p 47).

These lyrics combine several seemingly contradictory aspects of Jesus, who is meek and majestic, the sacrificial Lamb and the sin-conquering King, the suffering servant and the King of Glory. The overall focus of the hymn as we begin each stanza is on God's majesty.

Before we take a look at the lyrics of this hymn, we need to be certain we understand supremacy and majesty, particularly where it applies to God.

Psalm 8 begins (v 1) and ends (v 9) with the same proclamation:

> *O LORD, our Lord, how majestic is your name in all the earth! (ESV)*

The Psalmist refers to God as LORD by referring to His Hebrew Name "YHWH." This leaves out the vowels so that God's sacred Name, YAHWEH, is not misused. This Name for God was never spoken aloud.

---

[28] See "Who Composed the Tune *Hebron?*" on p 75.

In the New Testament Jesus is called "Lord," signifying that Jesus Christ is King of Kings and Lord of Lords. (Philippians 2:9-11). Therefore, as we use the word "majesty" to worship YWHW, we refer to the sovereign power, authority, greatness, splendor of quality, or character of God.[29]

Beginning the Psalm with this phrase, not only proclaims, but celebrates the omnipotence[30] of God and His authority over everything. God reigns supremely. There is no other power greater than His. Verses 2-8[31] of the Psalm speak of the attributes and universal work of God as proof for the final verse:

> O LORD, our Lord, how majestic is your name in
> all the earth! (ESV)

Throughout the hymn, we are led to experience not only the victory of Christ the King's coming, but also the seeming catastrophe or optical illusion[32] of His death on the cross.

---

[29] https://www.merriam-webster.com
[30] Ultimate authority, power.
[31] See "Supplemental Scripture Reading: Psalm 8:2-8" on p 71.
[32] Shirley's friend Sandy Wisdom-Martin's daughter coined the phrase "optical illusion" meaning that roadblocks come into our lives and totally occupy our thoughts, actions, and time and block us from seeing what is really happening.

These stanzas express several important aspects of the triumphal entry. Christ's riding to His death on a donkey is actually the beginning of Christ's triumph over death and conquering sin.

The majestic ride of Jesus into Jerusalem set into motion the events that led to His arrest, trial, forty lashes, crucifixion, death, burial, and victorious resurrection.

In the final stanza we sing about Christ coming to die in humility as He experienced excruciating pain.

Hallelujah, it does not end there! For at the end of the fifth stanza we sing that Christ will then take His power and reign.

Join us in singing.

Stanza 1
Ride on, ride on in majesty!
Hark! all the tribes hosanna cry;
O Savior meek, pursue your road
with palms and scattered garments strowed.

Stanza 2
Ride on, ride on in majesty!
In lowly pomp ride on to die:

O Christ, your triumphs now begin
o'er captive death and conquered sin.

Stanza 3

Ride on, ride on in majesty!
The winged squadrons of the sky
look down with sad and wond'ring eyes
to see th'approaching sacrifice.

Stanza 4

Ride on, ride on in majesty!
Your last and fiercest strife is nigh;
the Father on his sapphire throne
expects his own anointed Son.

Stanza 5

Ride on, ride on in majesty!
In lowly pomp ride on to die;
bow your meek head to mortal pain,
then take, O God, your pow'r and reign.

✚ You read, "we are led to experience not only the victory of Christ the King's coming, but also the seeming catastrophe or optical illusion of His death on the cross."

Describe how the death of Jesus on the cross was a "seeming catastrophe or optical illusion."

✟ The third stanza says, "The winged squadrons of the sky look down with sad and wond'ring eyes to see th'approaching sacrifice." (The "winged squadrons are the angels and "th'approaching sacrifice" is Jesus.) Explain why the angels were saddened as they saw Jesus approaching Jerusalem.

Implications of the Triumphal Entry for Addicts

If you have lived an addicted lifestyle, you have been duped. The empty promises that addiction offers of safety, freedom, a self-determined lifestyle, comfort, pleasure, possession of material things desired, autonomy, and more are all lies. These things might be experienced in a few fleeting moments, but the reality is that addiction enslaves and rules you.

Instead of providing safety, it offers you danger, especially in light of fentanyl and other drug overdoses. Instead of being free, you are a captive to your own passions and desires from within your own heart. You think you are wise enough to be in control, but you are really being held captive by your own heart desires. It is ironic to think that you have enslaved yourself, but it is YOU that has actually duped yourself. You believed the empty promises that ultimately failed to deliver.

But the promises of Jesus Christ are true, sure, and pure, and He can be trusted. He will not fool you. He is faithful to His Word which contains His promises to God's children. Just as He gave detailed instructions to two disciples to retrieve a donkey with its foal for His triumphal entry, you can believe His Word, even more than you can trust yourself. This is an important truth that the Bible teaches you: do not follow your feelings but choose to follow and obey God's commands over and above your opinions, ideas, and feelings. Some who struggle with addiction relapse after a lengthy period of sobriety simply because life's circumstances were not giving them what they wanted, wished for, or thought they deserved.

It is interesting that palm branches were waved at His triumphal entry because the people were torn in their belief of Jesus. While they knew He was the Messiah, they mistakenly believed Jesus would set up an earthly takeover to establish their ideas of what the Kingdom of God should be according to their opinions, ideas, and feelings. They were ready for a new government, and they were tired of the pagan culture surrounding them, so they shouted "Hosanna!" giving Jesus the glory as King and rightly so. But their expectations were still worldly; they wanted Him to fix their situation in their desired way.

If you have been living an addicted lifestyle, you may have looked to Jesus to save you in the way that you wanted to be saved and not in the way that the Bible tells you how and why God truly saves. God is faithful to fulfill His promises in the Holy Scriptures, so do not fool yourself into thinking He will be faithful to what you mistakenly believe to be a promise of His that He never actually made! Some believe that if they follow Jesus, they will never have a bad day, or any challenges, and the like. Yet God never promises life will be without pain or suffering. In fact, following Jesus is extremely difficult and painful at times. The reward comes in the next life and that is when God will remove your pain and suffering. In the meantime, there is much to celebrate in this life and much work for you to do to fulfill your God-given purpose. So, prepare your heart to celebrate and shout "Hosanna!" for the victory to come.

✟ You read about the empty promises addiction makes. What are some of those empty promises that have duped you?

✠ You read how the crowd was ready for a new government, and they were tired of their pagan culture, so they shouted "Hosanna!" giving Jesus the glory as King, and rightly so. But their expectations were still worldly; they wanted Him to fix their situation in their desired way.

Do an honest evaluation of why you want to have a relationship with Jesus Christ. Is it because you want Him to fix your situation in a certain way or do you truly desire to know and walk in obedience to Him? Write down your answer.

Day 5

Hymn of Response

How do we respond to Jesus who willingly rode a donkey into Jerusalem to die for us? We sing the majestic hymn *All Glory, Laud, and Honor* for which Theodulph of Orléans[33] wrote the lyrics that are sung to the tune *St.*

---

[33] See "Who Was Theodulph of Orléans?" on p 76.

Theodulph,[34] composed by Melchior Teschner. The hymn was translated from Latin to English by John Mason Neale.[35]

The hymn is based on the events of the triumphal entry. Today we remember and celebrate this as Palm Sunday. Before we look at this hymn, reread our Day 1 Old Testament Prophecy (p 46) and New Testament Fulfillment (p 47), paying particular attention to the instructions Jesus gave His disciples to *"Go into the village ahead of you. At once you will find a donkey tied there with her foal. Untie them and bring them to me. ³If anyone says anything to you, say that the Lord needs them, and he will send them at once"* (Matthew 21:2-3).

The disciples followed Jesus' instructions. In John's account of the triumphal entry, we learn that *His disciples did not understand these things at first. However, when Jesus was glorified, then they remembered that these things had been written about him and that they had done these things to him* (John 12:16). Do not miss the fact that everything about this was part of God's plan of redemption for mankind and had been foretold by the prophets. We read that

---

[34] See "Who Composed the Tune *St. Theodulph*?" on p 77.
[35] See "Who Was Johns Mason Neale?" on p 78.

these things *took place so that what was spoken through the prophet might be fulfilled* (Matthew 21:4).

After Jesus raised Lazarus from the dead, a crowd followed Him. This crowd was with Him as He traveled to Jerusalem. When they approached Jerusalem, a new crowd leaving the city joined them. Together, Jesus, His disciples and followers, and the crowd entered Jerusalem. *Then the crowds who went ahead of him and those who followed shouted: Hosanna to the Son of David! Blessed is he who comes in the name of the Lord! Hosanna in the highest heaven!* (Matthew 21:9)

When Jesus and the crowd entered Jerusalem, the city was in an uproar. Many asked who Jesus was. *The crowds were saying, "This is the prophet Jesus from Nazareth in Galilee"* (Matthew 21:11). Even though many in the crowd did not know that Jesus really was the Messiah, the excitement of the crowd spread among all those in the city. Through the hymn *All Glory, Laud, and Honor*, we express our praise and worship of Jesus similarly to how the crowds who escorted and welcomed Jesus into Jerusalem praised and worshiped Him.

The lyrics speak more fully of who Jesus is and what He did, than perhaps the crowds praising and worshiping

Him knew at the time. The hymn writer had a fuller understanding of God because He had access to the Bible, like we do today.

Join us in singing, as we proclaim that Jesus Christ is worthy of our praise and worship.

Stanza 1

All glory, laud, and honor

To You, Redeemer, King,

To Whom the lips of children

Made sweet hosannas ring.

You are the King of Israel

and David's royal Son,

Now in the Lord's name coming,

The King and Blessed One.

Jesus deserves our praise because He is our Redeemer, *who gave himself for our sins to rescue us from this present evil age, according to the will of our God and Father* (Galatians 1:4). He is also King of Israel and the seed of David. The writer of Hebrews[36] gives us more insight into who Jesus is and why He is worthy of our praise.

---

[36] See Supplemental Scripture: Hebrews 1:1-14" on p 72.

¹Long ago God spoke to the fathers by the prophets at different times and in different ways. ²In these last days, he has spoken to us by his Son. God has appointed him heir of all things and made the universe through him. ³The Son is the radiance of God's glory and the exact expression of his nature, sustaining all things by his powerful word. After making purification for sins, he sat down at the right hand of the Majesty on high (Hebrews 1:1-3).

Stanza 2

The company of angels

Is praising You on high;

And we with all creation

In chorus make reply.

The people of the Hebrews

With palms before You went;

Our praise and prayer and anthems

Before You we present.

God commanded His angels to worship Jesus Christ, as we read *when he brings his firstborn into the world, he says,* **And let all God's angels worship him** (Hebrews 1:6).

What a glorious sound of praise and worship the angels produced. Just imagine the beautiful sound when mankind and all of creation reply to the angel's praise with their own praise and worship of Him. We get a glimpse of this praise and worship as we read: *A very large crowd spread their clothes on the road; others were cutting branches from the trees and spreading them on the road. Then the crowds who went ahead of him and those who followed shouted:* **Hosanna to the Son of David! Blessed is he who comes in the name of the Lord! Hosanna in the highest heaven!** (Matthew 21:8-9)

Stanza 3

To You before Your passion

They sang their hymns of praise;

To You, now high exalted,

Our melody we raise.

As You received their praises,

Accept the prayers we bring,

For You delight in goodness,

O good and gracious King!

While during the triumphal entry the crowds were shouting, "Hosanna!" here we sing hymns of praise and worship. Because He receives our praise, we now ask that He accept, or hear, our prayers. *The LORD delights in those who fear him, who put their hope in his unfailing love* (Psalm 147:11 NIV).

✟ Today, God mainly speaks to us through His Holy Spirit-inspired Word. What commands or instructions has God given you through His Holy Spirit-inspired Word that you have found:

  ▪ easy to willingly obey?

  ▪ difficult to willingly obey?

✟ You read, "even though many in the crowd did not know that Jesus really was the Messiah, the excitement of the crowd spread among all those in the city." Explain the danger that following the crowd, like many of those around Jesus did, brings into our lives.

Prayer

Heavenly Father, thank You for using commonplace people and animals doing what You designed them to do—serve You in mighty ways. May we be cognizant[37] that we, like the donkey, are to simply do what we are made to do—serve You. In Jesus' Name, Amen.

Remember the Triumphal Entry

"He that was, as a rule, 'despised and rejected of men', was for the moment surrounded with the acclaim of the crowd. All men saluted Him that day with their Hosannas, and the whole city was moved. It was a gala day for the disciples, and a sort of coronation day for their Lord." – Charles Haddon Spurgeon

Prayers, Notes, & Questions

NOTE: If you need more room, see page 239.

---

[37] Knowledge of something, especially through experience. – MerriamWebster.com

Supplemental Scripture Reading

Matthew 21:7-17

⁷They brought the donkey and its foal; then they laid their clothes on them, and he sat on them. ⁸A very large crowd spread their clothes on the road; others were cutting branches from the trees and spreading them on the road. ⁹Then the crowds who went ahead of him and those who followed shouted: **Hosanna to the Son of David! Blessed is he who comes in the name of the Lord! Hosanna in the highest heaven!**

When he entered Jerusalem, the whole city was in an uproar, saying, "Who is this?" ¹⁰The crowds were saying, "This is the prophet Jesus from Nazareth in Galilee."

¹²Jesus went into the temple and threw out all those buying and selling. He overturned the tables of the money changers and the chairs of those selling doves. ¹³He said to them, "It is written, my house will be called a house of prayer, but you are making it a den of thieves!" ¹⁴The blind and the lame came to him in the temple, and he healed them.

¹⁵When the chief priests and the scribes saw the wonders that he did and the children shouting in the temple, "Hosanna to the Son of David!" they were indignant ¹⁶and said to him, "Do you hear what these children are saying?" Jesus replied, "Yes, have you never read: You have prepared praise from the mouths of infants and nursing babies?" 17Then he left them, went out of the city to Bethany, and spent the night there.

Supplemental Scripture Reading

Psalm 8:2-8 (ESV)

[2] Out of the mouth of babies and infants, you have established strength because of your foes, to still the enemy and the avenger. [3] When I look at your heavens, the work of your fingers, the moon and the stars, which you have set in place, [4] an that you are mindful of him, and the son of man that you care for him? [5] Yet you have made him a little lower than the heavenly beings and crowned him with glory and honor. [6] You have given him dominion over the works of your hands; you have put all things under his feet, [7] all sheep and oxen, and also the beasts of the field, [8] the birds of the heavens, and the fish of the sea, whatever passes along the paths of the seas.

Supplemental Scripture Reading

Hebrews 1:1-14

[1]Long ago God spoke to the fathers by the prophets at different times and in different ways. [2]In these last days, he has spoken to us by his Son. God has appointed him heir of all things and made the universe through him. [3]The Son is the radiance of God's glory and the exact expression of his nature, sustaining all things by his powerful word. After making purification for sins, he sat down at the right hand of the Majesty on high. [4]So he became superior to the angels, just as the name he inherited is more excellent than theirs.

[5]For to which of the angels did he ever say, **You are my Son; today I have become your Father,** *or again,* **I will be his Father, and he will be my Son?** *[6]Again, when he brings his firstborn into the world, he says,* **And let all God's angels worship him.** *[7]And about the angels he says:* **He makes his angels winds, and his servants a fiery flame,** *[8]but to the Son:* **Your throne, O God, is forever and ever, and the scepter of your kingdom is a scepter of justice.** *[9]You have loved righteousness and hated lawlessness; this is why God, your God, has anointed you with the oil of joy beyond your companions.*

[10]And: **In the beginning, Lord, you established the earth, and the heavens are the works of your hands;** [11]**they will perish, but you remain. They will all wear out like clothing;** [12]**you will roll them up like a cloak, and they will be changed like clothing. But you are the same, and your years will never end.**

[13]Now to which of the angels has he ever said: **Sit at my right hand until I make your enemies your footstool?** [14]Are they not all ministering spirits sent out to serve those who are going to inherit salvation?

Who Was Henry Hart Milman?

Henry Hart Milman[38] lived from 1791 to 1868 in London, England. He served as canon at Westminster, rector at St. Margaret's, and as Dean of St. Paul's. After his death, his hymns were published in *Heber's Hymns* (1827) and his own *Selection of Psalms and Hymns 1837.*

In addition to writing the lyrics for *Ride On, Ride On in Majesty*! he also wrote the lyrics for *O Help Us, Lord, Each Hour of Need*, and several other hymns.

---

[38] https://bit.ly/HHMilman

Who Composed the Tune *Hebron*?

Lowell Mason[39] lived from 1792 to 1872. He composed the tune *Hebron* to which *Ride On! Ride On in Majesty!* is sung.

After studying music and having his early compositions rejected, the Handel and Haydn Society of Boston, Massachusetts, accepted his compositions, without his name on them. He wrote a textbook to be used in singing schools, the first that presented a notation system that is unsurpassed to this day for clarity of statement, and orderly progressive arrangement.

In addition to composing the tune *Hebron*, he also composed the tune *Antioch* to which *Joy to the World!* is sung and *Hamburg* to which *When I Survey the Wondrous Cross* by Isaac Watts is sung.

---

[39] https://bit.ly/Lowell-Mason

Who Was Theodulph of Orléans?

Theodulph of Orléans[40] lived in Italy and France from 760 to 821. Although he was born into nobility, he chose to live a life in religious service. He served as abbot in Florence, Italy, and then Emperor Charlemagne appointed him Bishop of Orléans, France.

Louis the Pious, co-emperor with Charlemagne, imprisoned Theodulph inside cold stone walls on suspicion of loyalty to Italian leaders.

Sustained by his faith, Theodulph wrote *All Glory, Laud, and Honor*. He died in prison.

Theodulph is not known to have written any hymns other than, *All Glory, Laud, and Honor*.

---

[40] https://bit.ly/TheodulphOrléans

Who Composed the Tune
St. Theodulph?

Melchior Teschner[41] lived in Prussia and Posen (both now in Poland) from 1584 to 1635.

He studied philosophy, theology, as well as music under Bartholomäus Gesius at the University of Frankfurt an der Oder. He was a cantor and preacher, and pastor at Oberpritschen.

In addition to composing the tune *St. Theodulph,* he also composed the tune *Valet Will Ich Dir Geben,* to which *Rejoice, Rejoice, Ye Christians* is sung.

---

[41] https://bit.ly/MelchiorTeschner

Who Was John Mason Neale?

John Mason Neale[42] lived in England from 1818 to 1866. He was a prolific hymn writer. He also translated and adapted many old hymns.

He was influential in helping determine the architectural design of churches and cathedrals. He earned his Doctor of Divinity from Trinity College in Hartford, Connecticut.

In addition to composing the tune *St. Theodulph,* he also wrote the lyrics for *Good King Wenceslas.*

---

[42] https://bit.ly/JohnMasonNeale

The Lord's Supper

Begin Three Sundays Before Easter

Celebrate Easter This Week

Begin each day by confessing your sin and asking God to forgive your sin.

Pray your heart will be open to the correction, encouragement, and teaching of God's Word.

Pray the Lord will ignite your passion to know Him better and to understand the significance of the Lord's Supper in your life.

Take your time as you work through each day's reading to consider prayerfully and write out your answers to the exercises.

Day 1

Old Testament Prophecy

12 *"I will pass through the land of Egypt on that night and strike every firstborn male in the land of Egypt, both people and animals. I am the LORD; I will execute judgments against all the gods of Egypt.* 13*The blood on the houses where you are staying will be a distinguishing mark for you; when I see the blood, I will pass over you. No plague will be among you to destroy you when I strike the land of Egypt.* 14*This day is to be a memorial for you, and you must celebrate it as a festival to*

the LORD. *You are to celebrate it throughout your generations as a permanent statute"* (Exodus 12:12-14[43]).

[11]*"... They are to eat the animal with unleavened bread and bitter herbs;* [12]*they may not leave any of it until morning or break any of its bones. They must observe the Passover according to all its statutes"* (Numbers 9:11-12).

✟ Both of these passages are instances where God gave His people specific instructions to follow. In the Exodus passage, obedience to God's instructions saves the firstborn male children in the houses with blood painted on the doorpost. What commands (instructions) in the Bible do you find difficult to understand how your obedience will honor God and maybe save you from danger? Explain.

New Testament Fulfillment

[7]*Then the Day of Unleavened Bread came when the Passover lamb had to be sacrificed.* [8]*Jesus sent Peter and John, saying,*

---

[43] See "Supplemental Scripture Reading: Exodus 12:1-28" on p 102.

"Go and make preparations for us to eat the Passover." *9"Where do you want us to prepare it?" they asked him.* *10"Listen," he said to them, "when you've entered the city, a man carrying a water jug will meet you. Follow him into the house he enters. 11"Tell the owner of the house, 'The Teacher asks you, "Where is the guest room where I can eat the Passover with my disciples?"' 12Then he will show you a large, furnished room upstairs. Make the preparations there." 13So they went and found it just as he had told them, and they prepared the Passover* (Luke 22:7-13).

✝ The instructions Jesus gives Peter and John seem a little farfetched to us. Yet, Peter and John obeyed Jesus without any hesitation. Explain what motivated these men to follow Christ's seemingly farfetched commands without any hesitation. What motivates you to follow Christ's seemingly farfetched commands without any hesitation?

Symbol of Easter

Turn back to the chapter title page (p 79) and look at the illustration of the bread and the wine. These symbols represent elements of past and present celebrations. The Day 1 Old Testament Prophecy is about Passover.

Look back a little to see the history behind Passover. God told Moses to go to the Pharoah of Egypt and tell him to let His people—the Israelites—leave Egypt where they were enslaved. Pharoah refused nine times. Each time Pharoah refused to release the Israelites, and God sent nine plagues to Egypt, but Pharoah did not release the Israelites. The tenth time Pharoah refused to release the Israelites, God told Pharoah that He would strike down all the first-born sons in Egypt. God instructed the Israelites to paint blood on the doorposts of their homes, so that when God saw the blood, He would pass over that home, saving the first-born sons of the Israelites. (Read Exodus chapters 7–11.)

Passover is a memorial feast commemorating God passing over the homes of the Israelites. The blood painted on the doorposts also pointed to the atoning sacrifice of Christ, the Lamb of God.

As we continue looking at the events leading up to Easter, we see in the Day 1 New Testament Fulfillment (p 81) that Jesus and His disciples prepared for and observed Passover. The Passover and the Feast of Unleavened Bread were considered one celebration that was, and is, often referred to as the Feast of Unleavened Bread. These observances were memorials of when God spared the Israelite's first-born sons and saved the Children of Israel, so they could leave Egypt and head for the land God had promised them.

As Jesus celebrated the Passover meal (that we call the Lord's Supper) with His disciples, He gave new meaning to the Passover meal elements (bread and wine).

> [26]As they were eating, Jesus took bread, blessed and broke it, gave it to the disciples, and said, "Take and eat it; this is my body." [27]Then he took a cup, and after giving thanks, he gave it to them and said, "Drink from it, all of you. [28]For this is my blood of the covenant, which is poured out for many for the forgiveness of sins. [29]But I tell you, I will not drink from this fruit of the vine from

now on until that day when I drink it new with
you in my Father's kingdom." [30]After singing a
hymn, they went out to the Mount of Olives
(Matthew 26:26-30).

This new memorial focuses on Christ's sacrifice on the cross and leads us to remember His death. Today we call this the Lord's Supper, or Communion, during which Christ-followers remember the sacrifice of Jesus—His body and blood—that atoned for our sins. We eat unleavened bread,[44] the symbol that helps us remember the body of Jesus. We drink the wine (or juice), the symbol that helps us remember the shed blood of Jesus. As we eat and drink these symbols, we remember, renew, and declare our faith in Christ and His atoning sacrifice.[45]

Partaking of the Lord's Supper is something that we should not take lightly. Today we follow the example set by Jesus and the disciples as we prepare for the meal by carefully examining our heart motivations (1 Corinthians 11:28-29) and inviting the Holy Spirit to convict us of any unconfessed sin. When the Holy Spirit convicts us of sin,

---

[44] No leaven or yeast to make it rise.
[45] See "Supplemental Scripture Reading: 1 Corinthians 11:23-26" on p 105.

we must be quick to confess and repent of that sin before partaking of the Lord's Supper.

As we partake of the bread that represents Christ's body and the wine that represents the shed blood of Christ, we remember that Jesus told His disciples, *"Do this in remembrance of me"* (1 Corinthians 11:24). In 1 Corinthians 11:26 we read *"For as often as you eat this bread and drink this cup, you proclaim the Lord's death until he comes."* So, as we partake of the elements, the bread and wine, we remember the past—how Christ redeemed us.

The Lord's Supper is a celebration of being freed from the bondage of sin, including addiction, through the shed blood of Jesus Messiah. When we *eat* [the] *bread and drink the cup,* [we] *proclaim the Lord's death until he comes* (1 Corinthians 11:26).

This portion of the account ends with Jesus and the disciples singing a hymn and then going to the Garden of Gethsemane where Jesus prayed.

✝ The Lord's Supper serves as a memorial of Jesus giving His body and blood as a sacrifice to atone for our sins. Describe the thoughts and emotions evoked by considering your sins that were placed on Jesus as He took upon Himself the punishment through God's wrath that you deserved, He suffered, and died on the cross.

✝ The Lord's Supper is a celebration of being freed from the bondage of sin through the shed blood of Jesus Messiah. Describe the bondage of sin from which the shed blood of Jesus Messiah has freed you. If you have not been freed from the bondage of your sin, explain what is blocking you from that freedom. For help, talk with a trusted Christian friend who can help you understand how to be saved and set free from the bondage of sin.

Hymn of Easter

The hymn *In Memory of the Savior's Love* is not very well known. Thomas Cotterill[46] wrote the lyrics and Alexander R. Reinagle composed the tune, *St. Peter!*[47] in the early 1800s.

The hymn is based on 1 Corinthians 11:26, *For as often as you eat this bread and drink the cup, you proclaim the Lord's death until he comes.* Partaking of the Lord's Supper helps us focus our hearts and minds on why we eat the Lord's Supper.

Sing with us,

Stanza 1
In memory of the Savior's love
We keep the sacred feast,
When every humble, contrite[48] heart
Is made a welcome guest.

Here we express our understanding that the Lord's Supper is in memory of our Savior Jesus' love that He expressed as He *laid down his life for us* (1 John 3:16). In

---

[46] See "Who Was Thomas Cotterill?" on p 106.
[47] See "Who Composed the Tune *St. Peter?*" on p 107.
[48] Repentant.

humility, we prepare our hearts by examining them and asking the Holy Spirit to convict us of any unconfessed sin so we can confess and repent of that sin, receive forgiveness, and eat the supper in a worthy manner, which means sin is not hindering our communion with Him.

Stanza 2
By faith we take the bread of life
With which our souls are fed,
The cup is token of His blood
That was for sinners shed.

We eat the bread and drink of the cup by faith knowing our souls will be fed and nourished. The bread symbolizes the body of Christ, and the cup symbolizes the blood Jesus shed to save us from our sins. Our faith is strengthened as we remember the sacrifice Christ made on the cross so that we could be reconciled to God.

Stanza 3
Here let our ransomed powers unite
His honored name to raise,
Let grateful joy fill every mind,
And every voice be praise.

Eating the Lord's Supper is one form of praising God. Because He ransomed (redeemed) us, it is our joy to honor the Name of the One who saved us by praising and honoring Him and living a life of obedience to His Word.

Stanza 4

One fold, one faith, one hope,
One God alone we know;
Brethren we are; let every heart
With kind affections glow.

As we celebrate God's gracious gift of salvation that reconciled us to Him, the Lord's Supper unites Christ-followers. Ephesians 4:4-6 explains the unity Christ-followers experience with Him and each other, *There is one body and one Spirit—just as you were called to one hope at your calling—one Lord, one faith, one baptism, one God and Father of all, who is above all and through all and in all.*

Stanza 5

Beneath His banner thus we sing
The wonders of His love;
And here anticipate by faith
The heavenly feast above.

Being "beneath His banner" means we are saved, and we live under the Name and protection of God as we represent Him in everything we think, say, and do. The Lord's Supper is not just a reminder of what Jesus did in the past, it is a means by which we can have spiritual communion with Christ right now. The symbols of Christ's body (bread) and His blood (wine) point us to the communion Christ-followers will have in the future—eternity with Christ in heaven.

✞ In the second stanza we explain that "we eat the bread and drink of the cup by faith knowing our souls will be fed and nourished." This means our faith and walk with Christ is strengthened as we remember the atoning sacrifice of Christ on the cross. Describe in what ways your faith has been strengthened by remembering the atoning sacrifice of Christ giving His body and blood on the cross.

✞ Based on the definition you read of what "beneath His banner" means, describe how you live under the Name and protection of God as you represent Him in everything you think, say, and do. If you are not living "beneath His banner" explain what is keeping you from doing so.

Implications of the Lord's Supper for Addicts

God is faithful to His promises. He will bring to pass what He says He will do. Unlike addictive choices that have led you astray, choices to obey God, despite your own opinions, ideas, and feelings, might be difficult to execute, but will ultimately lead to spiritual blessings (not always material ones). Spiritual blessings may include any of the Fruit of the Spirit listed in Galatians 5:22-23: *But the fruit of the Spirit is love, joy, peace, patience, kindness, goodness, faithfulness, 23 gentleness, self-control. Against such things there is no law* (ESV). Why would you not want more love, joy, peace, patience, and the other fruit of the Spirit in your own life, and then share them with others?

The Passover as described in Exodus must have been as anxiety-provoking and exciting a time for the Israelites as almost any other time in their history. God sent ten plagues to the Egyptians who had enslaved His children which were designed as direct attacks on their belief in pagan gods (Exodus 12:12). The gods that they thought would deliver them were worshiped for a specific attribute. For example, the Egyptian goddess, Heket, was depicted with a frog head and was falsely believed to be responsible for providing life through the Nile River.

Well, what did God do? He sent a plague of frogs to overwhelm the land, they replicated, and went everywhere. They overtook homes and property in such a powerful and unusual way that God was sending a message that He was truly the One who had power over all His creation, including frogs and the Nile River. God sent plagues ten different times with ten different plagues to demonstrate His glory and power both to His children, the Israelites, and to the Egyptians, who had a false god for each type of plague God sent.

Living a life of addiction overtakes you. It overpowers you because you are not God, nor are you designed to be self-sufficient in this life. You need Jesus to save you, you need the Holy Spirit to indwell and to empower you, and you need God's Word of truth to battle the lies of the world and Satan. God allowed your addiction to overtake you so that you would look to Him rather than attempt to control it yourself. He wants to help you as you seek to obey and trust Him!

The Last Supper was an example of Jesus' obedience to the Father and a demonstration of His faith. He followed the custom, not because it was a custom, but because it symbolized something bigger in what God was doing. The same feelings of anticipation which occurred at the Passover were occurring during the Last Supper, yet the disciples were not fully aware of what was to come and was coming very soon.

To think that you are connected to His life and can inherit eternal life despite all that you have done, is a huge blessing and nothing to take lightly! This is why the Bible calls your choices in addiction a "sin," because God offers you forgiveness and newness of life when you confess your sin and trust Jesus as your Savior. Do not ever be afraid to confess your sinful opinions, ideas, attitudes, thoughts, feelings, beliefs, or actions because Jesus is ready and willing to forgive and cleanse you from all unrighteousness! There is Hope and the Last Supper is evidence that God is faithful to every word of His promises (Joshua 21:45).

✟ You read that our choices to obey God ultimately lead to spiritual blessings. Describe a time when you made a choice to obey God that ultimately led to spiritual blessings in your life and describe the spiritual blessings you received.

✝ Ask the Holy Spirit to convict you of any sinful opinions, ideas, attitudes, thoughts, feelings, beliefs, or actions. List the sins of which the Holy Spirit convicted you. Confess those sins to God and ask His forgiveness, then walk in the freedom of that forgiveness.

DAY 5

Hymn of Response

How do we respond when we remember that because of Christ's sacrifice and finished work on the cross, we are saved and able to commune with Him now and in the future? We go deeper and deeper in our relationship with Jesus.

Deeper and Deeper is a hymn for which Oswald Jeffrey Smith[49] wrote the lyrics and composed the tune. The hymn is about knowing Jesus in a deeper way. The Apostle Paul's prayer in Ephesians 3:16-19 was for the Ephesians to have a deeper relationship with God. He prayed that God would strengthen their spirits with power, and that through faith, Christ would dwell in their hearts. He continues praying that they would be *rooted and firmly established in love* and be able to comprehend the totality and fullness of God's love.

While Paul's prayer was a specific prayer for a specific people, it supplies instructions for how we can pray today, and it gives us some biblical principles which we can follow in our own lives.

Sing this prayer with us.

Stanza 1

Into the heart of Jesus

Deeper and deeper I go,

Seeking to know the reason

---

[49] See "Who Was Oswald Jeffrey Smith?" on p 108.

Why He should love me so—
Why He should stoop to lift me
Up from the miry clay,
Saving my soul, making me whole,
Though I had wandered away.

This stanza describes getting to know Jesus in a deeper way as we read, study, memorize, meditate, and contemplate upon His Holy Spirit-inspired Word. The deeper our knowledge and understanding of Jesus, the more cognizant we become of the depth of the Father's love for us.

Stanza 2

Into the will of Jesus
Deeper and deeper I go,
Praying for grace to follow,
Seeking His way to know;
Bowing in full surrender
Low at His blessed feet,
Bidding Him take, break me and make,
Till I am molded and meet.

In this stanza we pray for God's enabling grace to help us follow Him and know His will as we surrender our lives for Him to cull out all the sin and mold us into His image.

Stanza 3

Into the cross of Jesus
Deeper and deeper I go,
Following through the garden,
Facing the dreaded foe;
Drinking the cup of sorrow,
Sobbing with broken heart,
"O Savior, help! dear Savior, help!
Grace for my weakness impart."

This stanza reminds us of sharing the Lord's Supper. As we partake of the elements, we *proclaim the Lord's death until he comes* (1 Corinthians 11:26).

Stanza 4

Into the joy of Jesus
Deeper and deeper I go,
Rising, with soul enraptured,
Far from the world below;
Joy in the place of sorrow,
Peace in the midst of pain,
Jesus will give, Jesus will give,
He will uphold and sustain.

As we go deeper and deeper in our knowledge and understanding of God, we will experience His joy and peace, regardless of what is going on around us. He will uphold and sustain us.

Stanza 5

Into the love of Jesus

Deeper and deeper I go,

Praising the One who brought me

Out of my sin and woe;

And through eternal ages

Gratefully I shall sing,

"Oh, how He loved! Oh, how He loved!

Jesus, my Lord and my King!"

The deeper and deeper we go into the love of Jesus, the more we will praise Him—the One who saved us from our sin. The result of going deeper and deeper in our knowledge and understanding of Jesus is so that we *may be able to comprehend with all the saints what is the length and width, height and depth of God's love, and to know Christ's love that surpasses knowledge, so that you may be filled with all the fullness of God.* (Ephesians 3:18-19).

✞ The Apostle Paul prayed that the Ephesians would be *rooted and firmly established in love.* What are some ways

Christ-followers today can be *rooted and firmly established in love?*

✝ As we go deeper and deeper in our knowledge and understanding of God, we will experience His joy and peace. In what ways have you experienced God's joy and peace as a result of your deeper knowledge and understanding of Him?

Prayer

Gracious Heavenly Father, thank You for the honor of communing with You as we partake of the Lord's Supper. Give us a passion to go deeper and deeper in our relationship with You. In Jesus' Name, Amen.

Remember the Lord's Supper

"It is true that the Lord's Supper is only for sinners. But within that group, it is only for repentant sinners."
– Mark Dever

Prayers, Notes, & Questions

NOTE: If you need more room, see page 239.

Supplemental Scripture Reading

Exodus 12:1-28

¹The LORD said to Moses and Aaron in the land of Egypt: ²"This month is to be the beginning of months for you; it is the first month of your year. ³Tell the whole community of Israel that on the tenth day of this month they must each select an animal of the flock according to their fathers' families, one animal per family. ⁴If the household is too small for a whole animal, that person and the neighbor nearest his house are to select one based on the combined number of people; you should apportion the animal according to what each will eat. ⁵You must have an unblemished animal, a year-old male; you may take it from either the sheep or the goats. ⁶You are to keep it until the fourteenth day of this month; then the whole assembly of the community of Israel will slaughter the animals at twilight. ⁷They must take some of the blood and put it on the two doorposts and the lintel of the houses where they eat them.

⁸"They are to eat the meat that night; they should eat it, roasted over the fire along with unleavened bread and bitter herbs. ⁹Do not eat any of it raw or cooked in boiling water, but only roasted over fire—its head as well as its legs and inner organs. ¹⁰You must not leave any of it until morning; any part of it left until morning you must burn. ¹¹Here is how you must eat it:

You must be dressed for travel, your sandals on your feet, and your staff in your hand. You are to eat it in a hurry; it is the LORD's Passover. ¹²I will pass through the land of Egypt on that night and strike every firstborn male in the land of Egypt, both people and animals. I am the LORD; I will execute judgments against all the gods of Egypt. ¹³The blood on the houses where you are staying will be a distinguishing mark for you; when I see the blood, I will pass over you. No plague will be among you to destroy you when I strike the land of Egypt.

¹⁴"This day is to be a memorial for you, and you must celebrate it as a festival to the LORD. You are to celebrate it throughout your generations as a permanent statute. ¹⁵You must eat unleavened bread for seven days. On the first day you must remove yeast from your houses. Whoever eats what is leavened from the first day through the seventh day must be cut off from Israel. ¹⁶You are to hold a sacred assembly on the first day and another sacred assembly on the seventh day. No work may be done on those days except for preparing what people need to eat—you may do only that. ¹⁷You are to observe the Festival of Unleavened Bread because on this very day I brought your military divisions out of the land of Egypt. You must observe this day throughout your generations as a permanent statute. ¹⁸You are to eat unleavened bread in the first month, from the evening of the fourteenth day of the month until the evening of

the twenty-first day. ^{19}Yeast must not be found in your houses for seven days. If anyone eats something leavened, that person, whether a resident alien or native of the land, must be cut off from the community of Israel. ^{20}Do not eat anything leavened; eat unleavened bread in all your homes."

^{21}"Then Moses summoned all the elders of Israel and said to them, "Go, select an animal from the flock according to your families, and slaughter the Passover animal. ^{22}Take a cluster of hyssop, dip it in the blood that is in the basin, and brush the lintel and the two doorposts with some of the blood in the basin. None of you may go out the door of his house until morning. ^{23}When the LORD passes through to strike Egypt and sees the blood on the lintel and the two doorposts, he will pass over the door and not let the destroyer enter your houses to strike you. ^{24}Keep this command permanently as a statute for you and your descendants. ^{25}When you enter the land that the LORD will give you as he promised, you are to observe this ceremony. ^{26}When your children ask you, 'What does this ceremony mean to you? ^{27}'you are to reply, 'It is the Passover sacrifice to the LORD, for he passed over the houses of the Israelites in Egypt when he struck the Egyptians and spared our homes.'" So the people knelt low and worshiped. ^{28}Then the Israelites went and did this; they did just as the LORD had commanded Moses and Aaron.

Supplemental Scripture Reading

1 Corinthians 11:23-26

23For I received from the Lord what I also passed on to you: On the night when he was betrayed, the LORD Jesus took bread, 24and when he had given thanks, broke it, and said, "This is my body, which is for you. Do this in remembrance of me." 25In the same way also he took the cup, after supper, and said, "This cup is the new covenant in my blood. Do this, as often as you drink it, in remembrance of me." 26For as often as you eat this bread and drink the cup, you proclaim the Lord's death until he comes.

Who Was Thomas Cotterill?

Thomas Cotterill[50] lived from 1783 to 1826. He was a fellow at St. John's College, Cambridge. He served as curate of Tutbury, as incumbent of Lane End, Staffordshire, and as perpetual curate of St. Paul's, Sheffield.

In addition to writing the lyrics for *In Memory of the Savior's Love*, he also wrote the lyrics for *Awake, Ye Saints, Awake*, and several other hymns.

---

[50] https://bit.ly/TCotterill

Who Composed the Tune *St. Peter*?

Alexander Robert Reinagle[51] lived from 1799 to 1877. He composed the tune *St. Peter!* to which *In Memory of the Savior's Love* is sung.

He was organist at St. Peter's Church, Oxford, England. His uncle, also named Alexander, was a conductor, composer, and teacher in both Baltimore, Maryland, and Philadelphia, Pennsylvania.

In addition to composing the tune *St. Peter!* he also composed the tune *Ben Rhydding*, to which *My Soul Repeat His Praise* is sung.

---

[51] https://bit.ly/Reinagle

Who Was Oswald Jeffrey Smith?

Oswald Jeffrey Smith [52] lived from 1889 to 1986. He wrote twelve hundred hymns, Gospel songs, and poems. He served as a pastor in Toronto, Canada, from 1915 to 1959.

In addition to writing the lyrics and composing the tune for *Deeper and Deeper*, he also wrote the lyrics and composed the tune for *Jesus Only, Let Me See,* and several other hymns.

---

[52] https://bit.ly/OJSmith

I Don't Know the Man!

Begin Two Sundays Before Easter

Celebrate Easter This Week

Begin each day by confessing your sin and asking God to forgive your sin.

Pray your heart will be open to the correction, encouragement, and teaching of God's Word.

Pray the Lord will ignite your passion to know Him better and to boldly share about His gift of love, Jesus, with all those whom He brings across your path.

Take your time as you work through each day's reading to consider prayerfully and write out your answers to the exercises.

Day 1

New Testament Prophecy

No, this is not an error, today's prophecy is from the New Testament.

*30After singing a hymn, they went out to the Mount of Olives. 31Then Jesus said to them, "Tonight all of you will fall away because of me, for it is written: **I will strike the shepherd, and the sheep of the flock will be scattered.** 32But after I have risen, I will go ahead of you to Galilee." 33Peter told him,*

"Even if everyone falls away because of you, I will never fall away." ³⁴"Truly I tell you," Jesus said to him, "tonight, before the rooster crows, you will deny me three times." ³⁵"Even if I have to die with you," Peter told him, "I will never deny you," and all the disciples said the same thing (Matthew 26:30-35).

✝ Like Peter and the other disciples, we say we will never fall away from or deny Christ. However, our thoughts, words, attitudes, and actions often deny Him. List some of your thoughts, words, attitudes, and actions that deny Christ. Now take time to confess and repent for each instance you listed.

New Testament Fulfillment

⁶⁹Now Peter was sitting outside in the courtyard. A servant girl approached him and said, "You were with Jesus the Galilean too." ⁷⁰But he denied it in front of everyone: "I don't know what you're talking about." ⁷¹When he had gone out to the gateway, another woman saw him and told those who were there, "This man was with Jesus the Nazarene!" ⁷²And again he denied it with an oath: "I don't know the man!"

73After a little while those standing there approached and said to Peter, "You really are one of them, since even your accent gives you away." 74Then he started to curse and to swear with an oath, "I don't know the man!" Immediately a rooster crowed, 75and Peter remembered the words Jesus had spoken, "Before the rooster crows, you will deny me three times." And he went outside and wept bitterly (Matthew 26:69-75).

✝ Put yourself in Peter's place. Jesus had been arrested and Peter had joined a group in the nearby courtyard. Describe things you imagine might have been going on in Peter's mind that led him to deny Christ. Explain the doubts that arise in your heart which make you vulnerable to denying you know Christ.

Symbol of Easter

Turn back to the chapter title page (p 109) and look at the illustration. It depicts Peter sitting around the fire in the courtyard after Jesus was arrested in the Garden of Gethsemane.

Jesus and His disciples came to the Garden of Gethsemane together. He asked the disciples to wait and pray while He went farther into the garden to pray. Jesus knew the physical pain that He was going to experience, and, more importantly, He knew the spiritual agony He would experience taking on our sins and receiving the punishment and wrath of God we deserve for those sins. The agony of Jesus was so great that His sweat falling to the ground was like blood. (Read the entire account in Matthew 26:36-56.[53])

Judas brought soldiers into the garden and betrayed Jesus with a kiss. When the soldiers arrested Jesus and took him away, *all the disciples deserted him and ran away* (Matthew 26:56). Scripture tells us that Peter followed Jesus and the soldiers at a distance.

When the servant girl accused Peter of being with Jesus, Peter said he did not know what she was talking about. Basically, he denied knowing Jesus. A woman also accused Peter of being with Jesus, and Peter denied knowing Jesus again. Finally, bystanders accused Peter

[53] See "Supplemental Scripture: Matthew 26:36-56" on p 132.

of knowing Jesus and being with Him because he was Galilean like Jesus. Once again, Peter denied knowing Jesus (Matthew 26:57-73).

What happens next is horrifying to Peter. We read, *Immediately a rooster crowed, and Peter remembered the words Jesus had spoken, "Before the rooster crows, you will deny me three times"* (Matthew 26:74b-75a).

It is easy to read the accounts of Peter denying Christ and be a bit judgmental; right? Afterall, Peter was one of the disciples—those men who were closely associated with Jesus.

Turn back to the chapter title page (p 109) and look at the illustration again. Did you see the rooster on the wall by the column when you first looked at the illustration?

Have you noticed that when you sin, you often see or hear something that reminds you of God's Word and the Holy Spirit convicts you of your sin and leads you to repentance?

Jesus mentioned the rooster's crowing when he told Peter that he would deny Him. When Peter heard the rooster's crow, he immediately became aware of his sin. Someone said that when Peter heard the rooster's crow, it brought him back to himself, or it brought to Peter's mind what he had forgotten—that he loved and served Jesus. It reminded him of what Jesus had told him *and he wept bitterly* (Matthew 26:75b) in godly sorrow and repentance. Deep sorrow for our sin is evidence that our hearts have been transformed.

We sometimes are so fearful of what might happen to us that we, too, deny Christ. Maybe our denial is more subtle than Peter's, but it is denial, nonetheless.

We deny knowing Christ when we walk in fear of what others think of us or of what we think they may do to us or say about us, instead of trusting that God is with us and that He will enable us to walk through whatever we are facing.

Sadly, many times our social media posts or the way we treat others are ways we deny knowing Christ. Basically, any time we think, say, or do anything that disobeys God's Word, we deny that we know Christ. When we fail to think, say, or do what God's Word tells us to think, say, or do, we deny that we know Christ.

✝ You read how when we sin, we often see or hear something that reminds us of God's Word and the Holy Spirit uses that to convict us of our sin and leads us to repent. That is one of the reasons it is so important for us to read, study, memorize, contemplate, and meditate upon God's Word, so we know it and use Scripture to fight against temptations to sin. List some of the Scripture passages that can help you fight against temptations to sin.

✞ You read that we deny knowing Christ when we walk in fear of what others think of us or of what we think they may do to us or say about us. Describe a time when you were tempted to deny Christ because you feared what others would think of you or what you thought they might do to you or say about you.

Hymn of Easter

The little-known hymn *Peter's Denial* is a wonderful prayer that we would not deny Christ as Peter did. Philip Paul Bliss wrote the lyrics and the tune, *Maldives*.

Stanza 1

In the garden, boldly,

Peter would have fought;

Now he answers coldly,

Nay, I know Him not.

What a contrast we see here between the Peter with Jesus in the Garden of Gethsemane ready to fight the soldiers who came to arrest Jesus (John 18:10), with the Peter around the fire who quickly and coldly denied that He knew Christ. That sounds familiar to us, right? When we are surrounded by those whom we know and trust, we boldly step out to defend our friends and beliefs. Yet, when we are standing alone in a crowd of non-Christ-followers, we often not only refuse to defend our friends and beliefs, we also often deny even knowing them.

Refrain

I would stand forever
Near my Savior's side,
Lest to glory yonder
I should be denied.

The refrain is a proclamation of our intent to stand forever near the side of our Savior so that our entrance into heaven will not be denied. We will only spend eternity in heaven if we have been saved.

Stanza 2

Tho' life's stony pathway
Be with dangers fraught,
Let my falterings never
Say, I know Him not.

The second stanza is a prayer that even though our lives are comprised of paths that are difficult to walk upon, and are full of danger, we will not deny Christ by sinning. Thereby we signify to the watching world that we do not know Him as our Savior and Lord.

Stanza 3

Though long years of sorrow
Be my earthly lot,

Let my murmurings never
Say, I know Him not.

The third stanza is a continuation of our prayer that even though our lives are full of sorrow, we will not deny Christ through our complaining which shows our lack of faith and trust in Christ.

Stanza 4
In the dark temptation,
Vows and prayers forgot,
Let my yielding never
Say, I know Him not.

In the fourth stanza, we continue praying that when dark temptations cloud our faith and trust, and we forget the vows we made to God and the prayers we prayed that we would never deny knowing Christ. Again, this is so our thoughts, words, and actions will not show the world that we do not know Him. We pray that even though our lives are full of sorrow, we will not deny Christ through our complaining.

Stanza 5
So, in toil or pleasure,
Deed or word or thought,

Let me never, never,

Say, I know Him not.

In the fifth stanza, we end by praying that in everything we think, say, or do, the Lord will strengthen and enable us to never deny knowing Him, but to always live in a way that proclaims Him as our Savior and Lord.

✝ You read that when we are surrounded by those whom we know and trust, we boldly step out to defend our friends and beliefs. Yet, when we are standing alone in a crowd of non-Christ-followers, we often not only refuse to defend our friends and beliefs, we also often deny even knowing them. We have all been in situations with non-Christ-followers where we felt pressured to act or talk a certain way or to do certain things we knew were sinful. Explain how you can prepare yourself to stay strong and not be swayed by non-Christ-followers to think, say, or do sinful things.

✝ This hymn is a prayer that we would not deny Christ as Peter did. Write out your own prayer asking God to strengthen you so that you will not deny Him in anything you think, say, or do.

Implications of Denying Christ for Addicts

It is so easy to forget who you are in Christ and who He is in you! The cares of this world can overwhelm you if you let them, which is why you must be involved in a local church that not only preaches the Word of God, but also ministers to you in a personal, disciple-making way. Transformation from an addicted lifestyle into newness of life does not occur in isolation. In fact, the Bible warns us in Proverbs 18:1: *Whoever isolates himself seeks his own desire; he breaks out against all sound judgment.* (ESV) Isolation means that you will break *out against all sound judgment* where others will wonder, "What is wrong with her? Why is she acting so strangely? Why is she making such terrible decisions?" But when you run those wild and crazy ideas by someone who is a strong believer, knows the Word, and cares for you, you will often hear what you might not want to hear but need to hear: "No, dear one, that is a bad idea! Please don't do that!"

Notice that Peter was alone when he denied knowing Christ. Of course, this fulfilled Jesus' prophecy that Peter would deny Him three times before the rooster crowed. His denial ultimately had a redeemable, good purpose for Peter. Peter needed to fall so that he could see just how weak he truly was. Sometimes your pride makes you think that you can be clean and sober all by yourself, but you certainly need Jesus and His body, a local church.

Seek someone more mature in the faith to disciple you, too. This trusted Christian friend is someone you need to be completely honest with about everything. Rigorous efforts at being honest are what will help you to stay sober and to be transformed into Christlikeness so that you will fulfill God's purposes in your life. God saved you for good works (Ephesians 2:10) and He wants you to change and grow. His design for growth is not always easy and it is almost always relational, meaning you need a small group of people to love and shepherd you while you are on this earth. Remember Proverbs 27:17 says that relationships cause sparks to fly: *Iron sharpens iron, and one person sharpens another.*

The Bible is replete[54] with wisdom that encourages the honest and sometimes painful moments of true, biblical, and caring relationships that are not afraid to speak the truth in love to one another. Proverbs 27:5-6 encourages these types of relationships: *Better is open rebuke than hidden love. Faithful are the wounds of a friend; profuse are the kisses of an enemy.* (ESV) Open rebuke is telling someone publicly that they are incorrect according to God and His Word. Of course, it does not mean posting it on social media or yelling it from the rooftops, but the idea is that helping someone is not whispered but told in person and without fear. Rebukes are not personal. They are helping someone to see that their thoughts do not line up with God's Word. Yes, those are the *wounds of a friend*, but they are *faithful*, meaning you can count on them helping you when you allow them to do so.

Many of the addicted people we know get their feelings hurt when they are gently corrected. Do not allow yourself to be that sensitive or prideful! No one is above a rebuke. Though you might not like being rebuked, do not prefer the kisses of an enemy to the wounds of a friend.

---

54 Abundantly provided or filled. –MerriamWebster.com

Jesus allowed Peter to see how his pride and fear of man would lead him to deny Jesus. The same is true for you. Do not let your pride or fear of man (aka what others might think of you) cause you to give in to temptation and make sinful decisions to return to your drug of choice. This is the equivalent of denying Jesus, and it will only end in heartbreak, painful consequences, guilt, shame, and possibly even death. God wants you to know that you can tell Him anything because He can be trusted completely.

✝ We noted that Peter was alone when he denied knowing Christ. Describe a time when you were alone and your thoughts, words, and actions denied you knew Christ.

✝ Write down the name of one trusted Christian friend whom you can ask to be your trusted Christian friend. Explain why he or she will make a good trusted Christian friend.

Hymn of Response

What is an appropriate response when we recognize that our thoughts, words, and actions often deny that we know Christ? Like the Apostle Paul, we are to stand firm in our faith, as we stand up unashamedly and unafraid to declare that we know Christ and that we belong to Him. In Romans 1:16 we read *For I am not ashamed of the gospel, because it is the power of God for salvation to everyone who believes, first to the Jew, and also to the Greek.* In 2 Timothy 2:3, we read we are to *share in suffering as a good soldier of Christ Jesus* regardless of what is going on around us or what we fear may happen to us.

George Duffield, Jr.[55] wrote lyrics that are sung to the tune, *Webb,*[56] composed by George James Webb. This hymn is a call for us to *Stand Up! Stand Up for Jesus!* The stanzas teach us various aspects of what it means to "stand up for Jesus" or, how to keep from denying we know Jesus.

---

[55] See "Who Was George Duffield, Jr.?" on p 135.
[56] See "Who Composed the Tune *Webb*? on p 136.

This hymn reminds us that since spiritual battles are always going on within us and around us, we must be ready to fight at all times.

Join us in singing.

Stanza 1

Stand up, stand up for Jesus,

Ye soldiers of the cross;

Lift high His royal banner,

It must not suffer loss.

From victory unto victory

His army shall He lead,

Till every foe is vanquished,

And Christ is Lord indeed.

We are soldiers of the cross who must stand fast in our faith as we fight spiritual battles (see Ephesians 6:12). We are to let everyone know we are following Jesus as He leads us from one victory to another.

Stanza 2

Stand up, stand up for Jesus,

The solemn watchword hear;

If while ye sleep He suffers,

Away with shame and fear;

Where'er ye meet with evil,

Within you or without,

Charge for the God of battles,

And put the foe to rout.

Here we encourage each other to watch and pray to keep us from giving in to temptation that comes from outside of us, as well as from within us, from our own hearts and desires.

Stanza 3

Stand up, stand up for Jesus,

The trumpet call obey;

Forth to the mighty conflict,

In this His glorious day.

Ye that are brave now serve Him

Against unnumbered foes;

Let courage rise with danger,

And strength to strength oppose.

We are called through His Word (the trumpet call) to fight in the same way His trumpet called the Israelites to battle (Numbers 10:8-9).

Stanza 4

Stand up, stand up for Jesus,

Stand in His strength alone;

The arm of flesh will fail you,

Ye dare not trust your own.

Put on the Gospel armor,

Each piece put on with prayer;

Where duty calls or danger,

Be never wanting there.

As we sing, we are reminded that soldiers of Christ should never trust in our own strength or weapons. We must *be strengthened by the Lord and by his vast strength* and *put on the full armor of God so that* [we] *can stand against the schemes of the devil* (Ephesians 6:10-11). We put on each piece of armor with prayer so that wherever we are called or whatever danger we face, God will provide what we need to fight the battle. What a comfort!

Stanza 5

Stand up, stand up for Jesus,

Each soldier to his post,

Close up the broken column,

And shout through all the host:

Make good the loss so heavy,

In those that still remain,

And prove to all around you

That death itself is gain.

God has work for each of us to do (Philippians 1:21-22). Included in that work, is standing firm and encouraging each other.

Stanza 6

Stand up, stand up for Jesus,
The strife will not be long;
This day the noise of battle,
The next the victor's song.
To him who overcometh
A crown of life shall be;
They with the King of Glory
Shall reign eternally.

By faith we will overcome and receive the crown of life which is the symbol of victory as we read in Revelation 2:10, *Be faithful to the point of death, and I will give you the crown of life.* We shall reign eternally with Him in heaven as Revelation 22:3-5 tells us: *The throne of God and of the Lamb will be in the city, and his servants will worship him. ⁴They will see his face, and his name will be on their foreheads. ⁵Night will be no more; people will not need the light of a lamp or the light of the sun, because the Lord God will give them light, and they will reign forever and ever.*

✞ We read that since spiritual battles are always going on around us, and within us, we must be ready to fight at all times as soldiers of the cross who must stand fast in our faith. Describe ways you can be equipped and prepare yourself to be a soldier ready for the spiritual battles you will face.

✞ In the fourth stanza, we sing that we are to stand up for Jesus by standing in His strength alone because our own strength will fail us. Describe a time in your life when you tried to stand in your own strength and were knocked down or defeated.

Prayer

Gracious Heavenly Father, thank You that when we are in the midst of struggles and scary situations that You give us the enablement, strength, and armor to fight for our faith. In Jesus' Name, Amen.

Remember to Tell the World You Are a Christ-follower

"I'll tell the world, that I'm a Christian, I'm not ashamed, His Name to bear; I'll tell the world, that I'm a Christian, I'll take Him with me anywhere." – Baynard L. Fox, *I'll Tell the World That I'm a Christian*.

Prayers, Notes, & Questions

NOTE: If you need more room, see page 239.

Supplemental Scripture Reading

Matthew 26:36-56

³⁶*Then Jesus came with them to a place called Gethsemane, and he told the disciples, "Sit here while I go over there and pray."* ³⁷*Taking along Peter and the two sons of Zebedee, he began to be sorrowful and troubled.* ³⁸*He said to them, "I am deeply grieved to the point of death. Remain here and stay awake with me."* ³⁹*Going a little farther, he fell facedown and prayed, "My Father, if it is possible, let this cup pass from me. Yet not as I will, but as you will."*

⁴⁰*Then he came to the disciples and found them sleeping. He asked Peter, "So, couldn't you stay awake with me one hour?* ⁴¹*"Stay awake and pray, so that you won't enter into temptation. The spirit is willing, but the flesh is weak."* ⁴²*Again, a second time, he went away and prayed, "My Father, if this cannot pass unless I drink it, your will be done."* ⁴³*And he came again and found them sleeping, because they could not keep their eyes open.*

⁴⁴*After leaving them, he went away again and prayed a third time, saying the same thing once more.* ⁴⁵*Then he came to the disciples and said to them, "Are you still sleeping and resting? See, the time is near. The Son of Man is betrayed into the hands of sinners.* ⁴⁶*"Get up; let's go. See, my betrayer is near."*

⁴⁷*While he was still speaking, Judas, one of the Twelve, suddenly arrived. A large mob with swords and clubs was with him from the chief priests and elders of the people.* ⁴⁸*His betrayer had given*

them a sign: "The one I kiss, he's the one; arrest him." ⁴⁹So immediately he went up to Jesus and said, "Greetings, Rabbi! " and kissed him. ⁵⁰"Friend," Jesus asked him, "why have you come? " Then they came up, took hold of Jesus, and arrested him. ⁵¹At that moment one of those with Jesus reached out his hand and drew his sword. He struck the high priest's servant and cut off his ear. ⁵²Then Jesus told him, "Put your sword back in its place because all who take up the sword will perish by the sword. ⁵³"Or do you think that I cannot call on my Father, and he will provide me here and now with more than twelve legions of angels? ⁵⁴"How, then, would the Scriptures be fulfilled that say it must happen this way? "

⁵⁵At that time Jesus said to the crowds, "Have you come out with swords and clubs, as if I were a criminal, to capture me? Every day I used to sit, teaching in the temple, and you didn't arrest me. ⁵⁶"But all this has happened so that the writings of the prophets would be fulfilled." Then all the disciples deserted him and ran away.

Who Was Philip Paul Bliss?

Philip Paul Bliss[57] lived from 1838 to 1876. He wrote the lyrics for *Peter's Denial* and composed the tune *Maldives* to which this hymn is sung.

He was an itinerant music teacher who made house calls on horseback during the winter. He worked with musician Dr. George F. Root conducting musical institutes and composing Sunday School melodies. Evangelist Dwight L. Moody encouraged him to become a singing evangelist.

In addition to writing the lyrics and composing the tune *Maldives*, he also composed the tune *Ville du Havre* to which Horatio Gates Spafford's *It Is Well With My Soul* is sung.

---

[57] https://bit.ly/PPBliss

Who Was George Duffield, Jr.?

George Duffield, Jr.[58] lived from 1818 to 1888. He wrote the lyrics for *Stand Up! Stand Up For Jesus*.

Following the funeral of his friend, Dudley Tyng, Duffield preached a sermon tribute to Tyng that ended with a poem he wrote based on Tyng's dying words. We know the poem as the hymn, *Stand Up! Stand Up For Jesus*. He pastored churches in New York, New Jersey, Pennsylvania, Michigan, and Illinois.

In addition to writing the lyrics for *Stand Up! Stand Up For Jesus*, he also wrote the lyrics for *Savior, Like a Shepherd Lead Us*, and several other hymns.

---

[58] https://bit.ly/GDuffield

Who Composed the Tune *Webb*?

George James Webb[59] lived from 1803 to 1887. He composed the tune *Webb* to which *Stand Up! Stand Up For Jesus* is sung.

He was organist at the Boston Church of the New Jerusalem. Along with Lowell Mason, he founded the Boston Academy of Music and collaborated on their *Musical Library*.

His best-known tune, *Webb*, came from a secular song he wrote, *Tis Dawn, the Lark is Singing*.

In addition to composing the tune *Webb*, he also composed the tune *Let Every Heart Rejoice and Sing*.

---

[59] https://bit.ly/GJWebb

The Beautiful Cross

Begin One Sunday Before Easter

Celebrate Easter This Week

Begin each day by confessing your sin and asking God to forgive your sin.

Pray your heart will be open to the correction, encouragement, and teaching of God's Word.

Pray the Lord will ignite your passion to know Him better and that He will help you gain a deeper understanding of the finished work of Christ on the cross and the implications of that finished work in your day-to-day life.

Take your time as you work through each day's reading to consider prayerfully and write out your answers to the exercises.

DAY 1

Old Testament Prophecy

[4]Yet he himself bore our sicknesses, and he carried our pains; but we in turn regarded him stricken, struck down by God, and afflicted. [5]But he was pierced because of our rebellion, crushed because of our iniquities; punishment for our peace was on him, and we are healed by his wounds. [6]We all went astray like sheep; we all have turned to our own way; and the LORD has punished him for the iniquity of us all .... [10]Yet the LORD was pleased to

crush him severely. When you make him a guilt offering, he will see his seed, he will prolong his days, and by his hand, the LORD's pleasure will be accomplished. ¹¹After his anguish, he will see light and be satisfied. By his knowledge, my righteous servant will justify many, and he will carry their iniquities (Isaiah 53:4-6; 10-11).

✝ Describe your emotional reaction when you read that Jesus was *pierced because of our rebellion, crushed because of our iniquities*, so that we could have peace and be healed by His wounds.

New Testament Fulfillment

¹⁶*Then he handed him over to be crucified. Then they took Jesus away.* ¹⁷*Carrying the cross by himself, he went out to what is called Place of the Skull, which in Aramaic is called Golgotha.* ¹⁸*There they crucified him and two others with him, one on either side, with Jesus in the middle.* ¹⁹*Pilate also had a sign made and put on the cross. It said: JESUS OF NAZARETH, THE KING OF THE JEWS.* (John 19:16-19).

✝ If you are a Christ-follower, think about sinless Jesus being crucified and dying on the cross to pay the penalty for your sin. Write out a prayer expressing your thanks to Him for your salvation. If you are not a Christ-follower, read "Do You Know the Jesus About Whom You Have Been Reading?" on page 235. Also talk with a trusted Christian friend who can help you understand how to receive salvation through Jesus.

DAY 2

Symbol of Easter

Turn back to the chapter title page (p 137) and look at the illustration of Jesus hanging on the cross. What events brought Him to the cross? He was betrayed, arrested, and deserted by His disciples. He endured false accusations, Peter's denial, condemnation, beating, and mockery. Jesus was required to carry His own cross to Golgotha, where He was nailed to it. His cross was raised up into the air so that the weight of His body would suffocate Him. He was pierced in His side by a sword, then He died.

It is difficult to look at the cross when you understand the spiritual and physical suffering Christ experienced on it. So how can we call it a beautiful cross?

We often talk about the fact that, on the cross, Jesus took the sin of the world upon Himself. But do we really understand what that means? On the cross every sin—of every repentant person[60] who has lived, who lives now, and who will live until His return—was placed upon Him. Our finite minds cannot even imagine the horrible concentration of sin that was laid upon Him!

As a result of our sin, Jesus experienced something on the cross that no Christ-follower has ever, nor will ever, experience. *About three in the afternoon Jesus cried out with a loud voice,* **"Elí, Elí, lemá sabachtháni?"** *that is,* **"My God, my God, why have you abandoned me?"** (Matthew 27:46)

God the Father turned His back on His Son, Jesus, because God is too holy to look upon all our sin that was laid upon

---

[60] Person who confesses his or her sin, turns to God and turns away from that sin. –Dr. Howard A. Eyrich

Jesus. Here hung Jesus who had never committed sin, now covered with our sin.

This is a good time to back up just a bit. Sin came into the world through Adam and Eve.[61] God said the penalty for sin is death—spiritual and physical. On the cross, Christ paid the penalty we owed God for our sin. Jesus had to be fully God and fully man, in order to atone for all of our sin. It took a human being to pay for the sins of humanity. Since Jesus was fully God, He had the power to save us. And of course, He had lived a sinless life that enabled Him to stand in our place before God and receive the punishment and wrath of God that we deserved. Jesus gave Himself to atone for our sin *so that everyone who believes in him will not perish but have eternal life* (John 3:16b).[62]

After hours of suffering spiritual and physical anguish on the cross, John records that Jesus said, *"It is finished"* and then He died (John 19:28-30).

When Jesus declared *"It is finished"* He declared that He had completed the purpose for which God had sent Him to earth—to atone for our sin.

---

[61] See "Supplemental Scripture Reading Genesis 3" on p 159.
[62] See "Supplemental Scripture Reading John 3:13-21" on p 162.

Most often we think of beauty as something that is pleasing to the eye, so we think of the cross as the cruel instrument by which Jesus was crucified and died. We do not see its beauty. Beauty, however, is not always just those things that are pleasing to our eye. Instead, something is beautiful when it touches our hearts and transforms us. With this in mind, we can definitely see the intrinsic beauty of the cross on which God's sacrificial gift, His Son, Jesus, atoned for our sin. As we see the cross in our mind's eye, it magnifies the mercy, grace, and love of God, and we are drawn to its beauty.

✟ While God the Father will never turn His back on Christ-followers, we sometimes feel as though God has deserted us. Describe a time when you have felt as though God deserted you. What did you do to "shake" that feeling of being deserted?

✟ You read that "as we see the cross in our mind's eye, it magnifies the mercy, grace, and love of God, and we are drawn to its beauty." In your own words, describe how the mercy, grace, and love of God draws you to the beauty of the cross.

DAY 3

Hymn of Easter

There are so many theologically rich hymns about the cross. An Easter favorite of many people is *When I Survey the Wondrous Cross*. Isaac Watts[63] wrote these wonderful lyrics. Probably the best-known tune is the beautiful *Hamburg*,[64] composed by Lowell Mason. Another stirring tune to which these lyrics are sung is a traditional English tune, *O Waly, Waly*.[65]

This hymn is based on Galatians 6:14, *But as for me, I will never boast about anything except the cross of our Lord Jesus Christ. The world has been crucified to me through the cross, and I to the world.*

---

[63] See "Who Was Isaac Watts?" on p 163.
[64] See "Who Composed the Tune *Hamburg*?" on p 164.
[65] See "Who Composed the Tune *O Waly, Waly*?" on p 165.

The lyrics remind us that through the cross of Christ, we are consecrated, set apart for Christ. As the title *When I Survey the Wondrous Cross* suggests, we are to contemplate[66] what Jesus experienced on the cross. We know the details of His crucifixion from the Bible where we read all the accounts of Jesus' arrest, trial, beating, crucifixion, and actual death on the cross.

As we survey, or contemplate, the cross upon which Jesus died, we gain a deeper understanding of the depth of love that sent Him to the cross to take our sins upon Himself, to experience the wrath of God that we deserved, and to die in our place.

As you join us in singing, let the lyrics of this hymn lead your contemplation.

Stanza 1
When I survey the wondrous cross
On which the Prince of glory died,
My richest gain I count but loss,
And pour contempt on all my pride.

The more we understand what Christ did for us on the cross and how He atoned for our sins, we can view it as a wondrous and beautiful cross. The more we understand the depth of love and sacrifice the cross

---

[66] Mull over.

represents, the more grateful we become. This understanding leads us to say, along with the Apostle Paul, *everything that was a gain to me, I have considered to be a loss because of Christ* (Philippians 3:7).

Stanza 2

Forbid it, Lord, that I should boast,
Save in the death of Christ my God!
All the vain things that charm me most,
I sacrifice them to His blood.

Carrying on the theme from the first stanza, we sing that we have nothing to boast about except Christ's death that bought our atonement. Since Christ did all that was needed for us to have salvation, we must give up the vain[67] things we desire and give ourselves to Christ as a living sacrifice (Romans 12:1).

Stanza 3

See from His head, His hands, His feet,
Sorrow and love flow mingled down!
Did e'er such love and sorrow meet,
Or thorns compose so rich a crown?

The description of the blood as being sorrow (suffering) and love mingling and flowing down is a stunning picture. Jesus' suffering and death convey the limitless love of God that undergirds our salvation.

---

[67] Meaningless, possess no real value.

Stanza 4

His dying crimson, like a robe,
Spreads o'er His body on the tree;
Then I am dead to all the globe,
And all the globe is dead to me.

This verse was in Watt's original lyrics, yet, it is often omitted in hymnals. What a picture these lyrics paint. The crimson blood of Jesus covered Him like a robe as He hung on the cross. In response to His sacrifice, we must *put to death what belongs to your earthly nature: sexual immorality, impurity, lust, evil desire, and greed, which is idolatry* (Colossians 3:5).

Stanza 5

Were the whole realm of nature mine,
That were a present far too small;
Love so amazing, so divine,
Demands my soul, my life, my all.

Since we have surveyed and hopefully have a better understanding of the depth of God's love expressed through the crucifixion of His Son, we come to the realization that it is only by His grace that we have been saved (Ephesians 2:4-5). We recognize that even if we owned everything in nature it would not be enough to repay Christ for the gift of our salvation. The only thing we can give Him in response to His amazing and divine love, is everything—our souls, our lives, our all.

Stanza 6[68]

To Christ, who won for sinners grace
By bitter grief and anguish sore,
Be praise from all the ransomed race
Forever and forevermore.

Here we are recognizing that the finished work of Christ on the cross demands all Christ-followers to praise Him forever and forever.

✟ In the second stanza, we were reminded that since Christ did all that was needed for us to have salvation, we must give up the vain things we desire. List some of the "vain things" you desire. Write a prayer asking God to help you put off those vain things and put on godly things.

✟ In the fifth stanza, we are reminded that anything we could imagine giving to Jesus as a thank You or payment for His saving us, would not be enough to

---

[68] This stanza was not written by Isaac Watts. It appeared in several hymn compilations that were published between 1857 and 1875 but has not been included in most hymnals. See https://bit.ly/WhenISurvey_v6

repay Him. Yet, what He wants from us is everything — our souls, our lives, our all. What things do you need to do in order to give Jesus everything? If you are uncertain, ask a trusted Christian friend to help you understand how to give Him everything.

Implications of The Beautiful Cross for Addicts

From a human perspective, there is nothing beautiful in the cross. Jesus' death was so brutal and inhumane that no person should have ever suffered such a death no matter what their crime. Yet an innocent man suffered at the hands of sinners in a violent and wicked way so that God would be glorified, and His beauty could be known.

Mankind will never save. Addictive choices will never save you or truly relieve your pain. You might find temporary relief before your enslavement comes, but you are searching for the wrong things in the wrong places.

In that moment at Calvary, when God placed the sin of all mankind on His only begotten and sinless Son, God demonstrated His ability to bring another supra-logical concept to fruition: His justice and His grace occurring at the same time! God's justice was not downplaying the significance of sin and how ugly it is because His Son, your Savior, Jesus, took the disgusting brunt of our sins at the hands of wicked men who only mocked, sneered, and scoffed at Him (Luke 23). This was a picture of your sin, but it was so much worse than the Bible can convey to you, humanly speaking of course.

But God proves his own love for us in that while we were still sinners, Christ died for us (Romans 5:8). This is grace. Forgiveness of your sins through repentance and faith in Christ is a free gift to you (Ephesians 2:8-9), but it cost Jesus His sinless life in a way that He experienced excruciating pain and suffering until He commended His spirit into God's hands.

And then, it was finished. There is no further work that can or should be done. You can now rest from the sins of your past that might have plagued you. You can rest assured that your guilt and shame are covered by the blood of Jesus. Those sinful things you have done in your addictive past are now forgiven and are no longer what define you. Your identity now is different. You are a new creation in Christ (2 Corinthians 5:17). You are not simply recovering from an addiction by being a better version of your old self. No, instead, you are transforming like a caterpillar that becomes a beautiful butterfly who can fly and be carried along by the wind, except it is the Holy Spirit that carries you! This is transformation and it is found at the cross when you lay your sins at the feet of Jesus.

Celebrate Easter Sunday with the fervor you might have if your favorite team was in the Super Bowl or a championship game! Sing His praises! He is worthy of all your best praise. He is worthy of your life. Serve Him joyfully and exuberantly! You are no longer deserving of punishment on a cross but graciously and mercifully set free for the purpose of giving God your love and service to others for His glory alone.

✞ You read that "addictive choices will never save you or truly relieve your pain. You might find temporary relief before your enslavement comes but you are searching for the wrong things in the wrong places." Describe a situation when you sought to find temporary relief but realized that you were searching for the wrong thing in the wrong place.

✝ As a Christ-follower, you are no longer deserving of punishment on a cross but graciously and mercifully set free for the purpose of giving God your love and service to others for His glory alone. If you are a Christ-follower, describe ways you have been graciously and mercifully set free for the purpose of giving God your love and service to others for His glory.

If you are not a Christ-follower, read "Do You Know the Jesus About Whom You Have Been Reading?" on page 235. Also talk with a trusted Christian friend who can help you understand how to be graciously and mercifully set free for the purpose of giving God your love and service to others for His glory only.

Hymn of Response

How do we respond to God's incredible love that sent His Son, Jesus, to the cross to take upon Himself our sin as well as the punishment and wrath of God that we deserved? We sing the hymn, *The Love of God*, composed by Frederick Martin Lehman.[69] It points us to important truths about God's multi-faceted love for us. There are several Scripture verses that come to mind as we sing this hymn.

> *"For God loved the world in this way: He gave his one and only Son, so that everyone who believes in him will not perish but have eternal life"* (John 3:16).

> [35]*Who can separate us from the love of Christ? Can affliction or distress or persecution or famine or nakedness or danger or sword? …* [37]*No, in all these things we are more than conquerors through him who loved us.* [38]*For I am persuaded that neither death nor life, nor angels nor rulers, nor things present nor things to come, nor powers,* [39]*nor height nor depth, nor any other created thing will*

---

[69] See "Who Was Frederick Martin Lehman?" on p 166.

153

be able to separate us from the love of God that is in Christ Jesus our Lord (Romans 8:35, 37-39).

Join us in singing about the love of God.

Stanza 1

The love of God is greater far
Than tongue or pen can ever tell;
It goes beyond the highest star,
And reaches to the lowest hell;
The guilty pair, bowed down with care,
God gave His Son to win;
His erring child He reconciled,
And pardoned from his sin.

Here we acknowledge that God's love is greater than anything we can talk or write about. God *proves his own love for us in that while we were still sinners, Christ died for us* (Romans 5:8) so that our sins would be forgiven, and we would be reconciled to Him.

Refrain

O love of God, how rich and pure!
How measureless and strong!
It shall forevermore endure
The saints' and angels' song.

The refrain reiterates the greatness, strength, and eternality of God's love. Nothing we know or experience supersedes the love of God.

Stanza 2

When hoary[70] time shall pass away,
And earthly thrones and kingdoms fall,
When men who here refuse to pray,
On rocks and hills and mountains call,
God's love so sure, shall still endure,
All measureless and strong;
Redeeming grace to Adam's race —
The saints' and angels' song.

Here we remind ourselves that when the last days on earth arrive, those who have not believed in God and have refused to pray to Him will beg the mountains and hills to fall on and over them (Luke 23:30). Even so, God's love is durable and sure. Motivated by love, God will continue redeeming sinful man to Himself. God's love is mighty enough to redeem the entire human race.

Stanza 3

Could we with ink the ocean fill,
And were the skies of parchment made,

---

[70] Old age or years of time.

Were every stalk on earth a quill,

And every man a scribe by trade;

To write the love of God above

Would drain the ocean dry;

Nor could the scroll contain the whole,

Though stretched from sky to sky.

The third stanza lyrics of this Jewish poem were found in an insane asylum, written on the wall of a patient's room after he was carried to his grave. Most people agree these words could have only been written in his scarce moments of sanity.

What a splendid expression of our inability to fully describe the love of God! Nothing is greater than God's love. It is strong to save, to strengthen, and to endure forever.

Regardless of the situations that we may encounter in our lives, the love of God is greater and more powerful than any of them!

✝ We know that "regardless of the situations that we may encounter in our lives, the love of God is greater and more powerful than any of them!"

Describe a situation in your life where you experience the love of God gives you encouragement for today and for your future.

✝ The whole point of this hymn is that God's love is so great that we can never fully describe His love. Take a few moments to think about God's love and in your own words, write a brief description of His love.

Prayer

Gracious Heavenly Father, thank You for the beautiful cross by which we glimpse Your mercy, grace, and love as You gave Your Son to be the sacrifice for our sin. May Christ's sacrifice for us compel and propel us to share the Good News of Christ with all those whom You bring across our path. In Jesus' Name, Amen.

Remember the Beautiful Cross

"God, through the shed blood of His Son, Jesus, redeems the lives of those who trust in Him from eternal damnation and wrath by bringing us into His family and calling us His children." – Shirley Crowder[71]

Prayers, Notes, & Questions

NOTE: If you need more room, see page 239.

---

[71] *Glimpses of God: a spring devotion for women*, Shirley Crowder and Harriet E. Michael, 2021.

Supplemental Scripture Reading

Genesis 3

[1]*Now the serpent was the most cunning of all the wild animals that the LORD God had made. He said to the woman, "Did God really say, 'You can't eat from any tree in the garden'?"* [2]*The woman said to the serpent, "We may eat the fruit from the trees in the garden.* [3]*"But about the fruit of the tree in the middle of the garden, God said, 'You must not eat it or touch it, or you will die.'"* [4]*"No! You will not die," the serpent said to the woman.* [5]*"In fact, God knows that when you eat it your eyes will be opened and you will be like God, knowing good and evil."* [6]*The woman saw that the tree was good for food and delightful to look at, and that it was desirable for obtaining wisdom. So she took some of its fruit and ate it; she also gave some to her husband, who was with her, and he ate it.* [7]*Then the eyes of both of them were opened, and they knew they were naked; so they sewed fig leaves together and made coverings for themselves*

[8]*Then the man and his wife heard the sound of the LORD God walking in the garden at the time of the evening breeze, and they hid from the LORD God among the trees of the garden.* [9]*So the LORD God called out to the man and said to him, "Where are you?"* [10]*And he said, "I heard you in the garden, and I was afraid because I was naked, so I hid."* [11]*Then he asked, "Who told you that you were naked? Did you eat from the tree that I commanded you not to eat from?"* [12]*The man replied, "The woman you gave to be with me—she gave me some fruit from*

the tree, and I ate." ¹³So the LORD God asked the woman, "What is this you have done?" And the woman said, "The serpent deceived me, and I ate."

¹⁴So the LORD God said to the serpent: Because you have done this, you are cursed more than any livestock and more than any wild animal. You will move on your belly and eat dust all the days of your life. ¹⁵I will put hostility between you and the woman, and between your offspring and her offspring. He will strike your head, and you will strike his heel.

¹⁶He said to the woman: I will intensify your labor pains; you will bear children with painful effort. Your desire will be for your husband, yet he will rule over you.

¹⁷And he said to the man, "Because you listened to your wife and ate from the tree about which I commanded you, 'Do not eat from it': The ground is cursed because of you. You will eat from it by means of painful labor all the days of your life. ¹⁸"It will produce thorns and thistles for you, and you will eat the plants of the field. ¹⁹"You will eat bread by the sweat of your brow until you return to the ground, since you were taken from it. For you are dust, and you will return to dust."

²⁰The man named his wife Eve because she was the mother of all the living. ²¹The LORD God made clothing from skins for the man and his wife, and he clothed them. ²²The LORD God said, "Since the man has become like one of us, knowing good and evil, he must not reach out, take from the tree of life, eat, and live forever."

²³So the LORD God sent him away from the garden of Eden to work the ground from which he was taken. ²⁴He drove the man out and stationed the cherubim and the flaming, whirling sword east of the garden of Eden to guard the way to the tree of life.

Supplemental Scripture Reading

John 3:13-21

13"No one has ascended into heaven except the one who descended from heaven—the Son of Man. 14"Just as Moses lifted up the snake in the wilderness, so the Son of Man must be lifted up, 15so that everyone who believes in him may have eternal life. 16For God loved the world in this way: He gave his one and only Son, so that everyone who believes in him will not perish but have eternal life. 17For God did not send his Son into the world to condemn the world, but to save the world through him. 18Anyone who believes in him is not condemned, but anyone who does not believe is already condemned, because he has not believed in the name of the one and only Son of God. 19This is the judgment: The light has come into the world, and people loved darkness rather than the light because their deeds were evil. 20For everyone who does evil hates the light and avoids it, so that his deeds may not be exposed. 21But anyone who lives by the truth comes to the light, so that his works may be shown to be accomplished by God."

Who Was Isaac Watts?

Isaac Watts[72] lived in England from 1674 to 1748. He learned Greek, Latin, and Hebrew as a child. Although he wrote and published many sermons, treatises, poems, and hymns, he is probably best known as a writer of hymns and paraphrases of various Psalms.

In addition to *When I Survey the Wondrous Cross*, he also wrote the wonderful hymn, *Alas, and Did My Savior Bleed* and hundreds more hymns.

---

[72] https://bit.ly/Isaac-Watts

Who Composed the Tune *Hamburg*?

Lowell Mason[73] lived from 1792 to 1872. He composed the tune *Hamburg* to which *When I Survey the Wondrous Cross* is sung.

After studying music and having his early compositions rejected, the Handel and Haydn Society of Boston, Massachusetts, accepted his compositions without his name on them. He wrote a textbook to be used in singing schools, the first that presented a notation system that is unsurpassed to this day for clarity of statement, and orderly progressive arrangement.

In addition to composing the tune *Hamburg*, he also composed the tune *Antioch* to which *Joy to the World!* is sung.

---

[73] https://bit.ly/Lowell-Mason

Who Composed the Tune
O Waly, Waly?

The beautiful tune *O Waly, Waly* has a long history. We do not know when the first version was composed or by whom it was composed. It is said to be a Scottish Air and began appearing in secular music publications in the early 1700s.

The tune was collected by and popularized in 1906 by Cecil Sharp. It was combined with the lyrics *The Water is High*.

This beautiful tune we now know as *O Waly, Waly*, has been revised numerous times.

Who Was Frederick Martin Lehman?

Frederick Martin Lehman[74] lived from 1868 to 1953. He was born in Germany and emigrated to America with his family when he was four years old. He served pastorates in Iowa, Indiana, and Missouri. Lehman helped establish the Nazarene Publishing House.

In addition to *The Love of God*, he also wrote the wonderful hymn, *There's No Disappointment in Heaven*, and hundreds of songs and several other hymns.

---

[74] https://bit.ly/FMLehman

He Is Risen, Indeed!

Begin Easter Sunday

Celebrate Easter This Week

Begin each day by confessing your sin and asking God to forgive your sin.

Pray your heart will be open to the correction, encouragement, and teaching of God's Word.

Pray the Lord will ignite your passion to know Him better as you meditate on the significance of the resurrection of Christ in your life.

Take your time as you work through each day's reading to consider prayerfully and write out your answers to the exercises.

DAY 1

Old Testament Prophecy

[9]Yet the LORD was pleased to crush him severely. When you make him a guilt offering, he will see his seed, he will prolong his days, and by his hand, the LORD's pleasure will be accomplished (Isaiah 53:10).[75]

✝ This prophecy not only speaks of Christ's death as a guilt offering, but of His resurrection as He will see

---

[75] See "Supplemental Scripture Isaiah 53:1-12" on p 194.

those whom He has redeemed. Jesus as a guilt offering bore the sin of every repentant person who has ever lived and those who will live until Christ's return. Write a prayer thanking Jesus for bearing the guilt for your sins that were laid on Him. If you have not come to a saving knowledge of Jesus, read "Do You Know the Jesus About Whom You Have Been Reading?" on page 235. Also talk with a trusted Christian friend who can help you understand how to be redeemed (saved) through Christ's death and resurrection.

Jesus' Prophecy

"For as Jonah [see Jonah 1:17] *was in the belly of the huge fish three days and three nights, so the Son of Man will be in the heart of the earth three days and three nights* (Matthew 12:40).

[22]*As they were gathering together in Galilee, Jesus told them, "The Son of Man is about to be betrayed into the hands of men.* [23]*They will kill him, and on the third day he will be raised up. And they were deeply distressed* (Matthew 17:22-23).

✟ The disciples were *deeply distressed* to hear that Jesus was going to be betrayed and killed. It seems as though they focused on this, instead of the fact that He would arise on the third day. Put yourself in the place of the disciples. Describe what emotions you think they might have been experiencing.

New Testament Fulfillment

"He is not here. For he has risen, just as he said. Come and see the place where he lay" (Matthew 28:6).[76]

³For I passed on to you as most important what I also received: that Christ died for our sins according to the Scriptures, ⁴that he was buried, that he was raised on the third day according to the Scriptures, ⁵and that he appeared to Cephas, then to the Twelve. ⁶Then he appeared to over five hundred brothers and sisters at one time; most of them are still alive, but some have fallen asleep. ⁷Then he appeared to James, then to all the apostles. ⁸Last of all, as to one born at the wrong time, he also appeared to me. ⁹For I

---

[76] See "Supplemental Scripture Matthew 28:1-6" on p 196.

am the least of the apostles, not worthy to be called an apostle, because I persecuted the church of God (1 Corinthians 15:3-9).

✝ Paul ends this portion of Scripture by saying he is *not worthy to be called an apostle,* because he persecuted the church of God. Remember that before His conversion, Paul killed Christ-followers. This means that Paul is cognizant that he was saved by God's mercy and grace alone. He knew he did nothing to deserve that mercy and grace. Describe how you have experienced God's mercy and grace in your life. If you have not experienced God's mercy and grace, read "Do You Know the Jesus About Whom You Have Been Reading?" on page 235. Also talk with a trusted Christian friend who can help you understand how to experience God's saving mercy and grace.

Symbol of Easter

Turn back to the chapter title page (p 167) and look at the illustration. This depicts what it could have looked like from inside the tomb after Christ arose. You will note the graves clothes are folded and the stone rolled away from the entrance.

Picking up where we were in the biblical account of His life, we see Jesus on the cross ... dead. The imprint of Jesus' excruciating death and sacrifice on the cross is indelibly burned in our hearts and minds, bringing on a myriad of contrasting emotions. We experience deep sorrow as we recognize that it was our sin which Jesus died to atone. Almost simultaneously we experience ecstatic joy which manifests itself in praise and worship as we realize that through His sacrifice, our sins are forgiven.

When Jesus died, the curtain entrance to The Most Holy Place (Holy of Holies)[77] in the temple *was torn in two from top to bottom, the earth quaked, and the rocks were split.* Then

---

[77] The place in the Temple where the Ark of the Covenant and the cherubim were. It was separated by an embroidered veil that blocked the view of the Ark and the cherubim. Only the High Priest could enter once a year on the Day of Atonement to make an annual sacrifice to atone for the sins of the repentant Israelites.

we read *When the centurion and those with him, who were keeping watch over Jesus, saw the earthquake and the things that had happened, they were terrified and said, "Truly this man was the Son of God!"* (Matthew 27:51-54) After Joseph of Arimathea asked Pilate for Jesus' body, Pilate allowed him to take Jesus down from the cross. Joseph wrapped His body in linen and placed Him in his own tomb which was cut into rock. Before leaving the tomb, Joseph rolled a large stone against the entrance (Matthew 27:57-61).

Many people mistakenly presumed Jesus would build an earthly empire and become a human king of Israel, even though He had told them that He would die (Matthew 17:22-23). Christ's disciples and followers were shocked, saddened, confused, and they wept bitterly because they thought Jesus' life had ended.

Everyone had forgotten the Day 1 Old Testament Prophecy that told us God the Father was pleased with the finished work of Jesus Messiah on the cross, by which the world could be reconciled to Himself.

They had also forgotten the Day 1 Jesus' Prophecy where He told them He would be killed and raised from the dead in three days.

They did not understand that Jesus was the King of Kings; nor did they understand that Jesus would become the High Priest pleading with God on their behalf.

The time between the crucifixion and the resurrection serves as a good reminder for us today. When things in our lives fall apart, we, like the disciples and followers of Jesus, are shocked, saddened, and confused. We weep bitterly and allow our circumstances to control our thoughts and emotions.

During these times we must remind ourselves of what we know to be true—God is sovereign in everything. We must take our eyes off the chaos around us and keep them on Jesus who will walk beside us or carry us through whatever we are experiencing.

Mark 16:1-8 gives us the continuing account.[78]

> *1When the Sabbath was over, Mary Magdalene, Mary the mother of James, and Salome bought spices, so that they could go and anoint him. 2Very early in the morning, on the first day of the week, they went to the tomb at sunrise. 3They were saying to one another, "Who will roll away the*

---

[78] See "Supplemental Scripture Reading: Luke 24:1-12" on p 197 for another account.

stone from the entrance to the tomb for us?"
*⁴Looking up, they noticed that the stone—which
was very large—had been rolled away.*

*⁵When they entered the tomb, they saw a young
man dressed in a white robe sitting on the right
side; they were alarmed. ⁶"Don't be alarmed," he
told them. "You are looking for Jesus of Nazareth,
who was crucified. He has risen! He is not here.
See the place where they put him. ⁷"But go, tell his
disciples and Peter, 'He is going ahead of you to
Galilee; you will see him there just as he told you.'"
⁸They went out and ran from the tomb, because
trembling and astonishment overwhelmed them.
And they said nothing to anyone, since they were
afraid.*

When Jesus rose victorious over the grave, God's mercy
and grace were manifested to reconcile us to Him for
eternity.

Regardless of what we have been through in our past,
what we are dealing with today, or what the future holds,
we can rejoice and say, "He is risen!"

How can we rejoice? We can rejoice because Jesus
conquered sin, death, and the cross. We can face anything

in our past, present, and future, with His enabling grace and mercy.

On Easter Sunday, our excitement increases as we joyfully celebrate Resurrection Day. Among Christ-followers and in many churches all over the world and through the ages, we hear the proclamation, "He is risen!" The enthusiastic response of Christ-followers is "He is risen, indeed!"

☩ We read that "the imprint of Jesus' excruciating death and sacrifice on the cross is indelibly burned in our hearts and minds, bringing on a myriad of contrasting emotions." When you think about Jesus' death and sacrifice: describe the sorrow you experience and describe the ways your joy manifests itself in praise and worship.

☩ We read "when things in our lives fall apart, we, like the disciples and followers of Jesus, are shocked, saddened, and confused. We weep bitterly and allow our circumstances to control our thoughts and emotions." Describe a time when things in your life fell apart and you were shocked, saddened, and confused. Explain how God enabled you to keep your eyes on Him rather than the chaos around you.

DAY 3

Hymn of Easter

The most popular Easter hymn in the English language is *Christ the Lord is Risen Today*. Charles Wesley[79] wrote the lyrics. The composer of the tune, *Easter Hymn*,[80] is unknown.

This theologically rich hymn celebrates the resurrection of Jesus Christ. It leads us to engage our hearts, souls, and minds with the passionate language that helps us experience the significance of the death, burial, and resurrection of our Savior and Lord, Jesus Messiah.

---

[79] See "Who Was Charles Wesley?" on p 198.
[80] See "Who Composed the Tune *Easter Hymn*? on p 199.

Two Scripture passages relating to this hymn come to mind, Matthew 28:5-6:

> [5]*The angel told the women, "Don't be afraid, because I know you are looking for Jesus who was crucified.* [6]*"He is not here. For he has risen, just as he said. Come and see the place where he lay.*

and 1 Corinthians 15:20.

> *But as it is, Christ has been raised from the dead, the firstfruits of those who have fallen asleep.*

This hymn is about mankind's relationship with God as He transforms us into His image. The "Alleluia!" at the end of each proclamation gives us an opportunity to respond to each one by praising Him.

Join us in celebrating the transforming work of God in our lives as we sing.

Stanza 1

Christ the Lord is ris'n today, Alleluia!

Sons of men and angels say, Alleluia!

Raise your joys and triumphs high, Alleluia!

Sing, ye heav'ns, and earth, reply, Alleluia!

Here we proclaim boldly the truth that because Christ rose from the dead, he *was appointed to be the powerful Son of God according to the Spirit of holiness by the resurrection of the dead* (Romans 1:4). Our response to the risen Christ is to praise Him.

Stanza 2

Love's redeeming work is done, Alleluia!
Fought the fight, the battle won, Alleluia!
Death in vain forbids His rise, Alleluia!
Christ hath opened paradise, Alleluia!

On the cross, Jesus said, *"It is finished."* He meant that He had finished the work His Father had sent Him to do—redeem sinners! As we sing the third line of this stanza, we are reminded that death tried in vain to stop Christ, but He won the victory over death.

Stanza 3

Vain the stone, the watch, the seal, Alleluia!
Christ hath burst the gates of hell, Alleluia!
Death in vain forbids its rise, Alleluia!
Christ has opened paradise, Alleluia!

Here we sing of how the stone that sealed the tomb and the guards who were ordered to watch the tomb were made ineffective when Christ arose and defeated death

(Matthew 27:59-28:2). Through His resurrection, Christ-followers are assured of eternal life with Him in heaven (paradise).

Stanza 4

Lives again our glorious King, Alleluia!

Where, O death, is now thy sting? Alleluia!

Once He died our souls to save, Alleluia!

Where thy victory, O grave? Alleluia!

Because of Christ's resurrection, we do not have to fear death nor the grave because *Death has been swallowed up in victory. Where, death, is your victory? Where, death, is your sting?* (1 Corinthians 15:54-55). Christ-followers will conquer death when we are raised with Him.

Stanza 5

Soar we now where Christ hath led, Alleluia!

Foll'wing our exalted Head, Alleluia!

Made like Him, like Him we rise, Alleluia!

Ours the cross, the grave, the skies, Alleluia!

Sadly, this stanza is sometimes omitted in hymn books. Here we sing that because Christ is risen from the dead, we can have Hope as we follow our "exalted Head" Jesus. We will be like Him and live with Him for eternity (Philippians 3:20-21).

Stanza 6

What tho' once we perished all, Alleluia!

Partners in our parents' fall, Alleluia!

Second life we all receive, Alleluia!

In our heav'nly Adam live, Alleluia!

We sing of what we were before we came to Christ, *dead in our trespasses and sins* (Ephesians 2:1). We were "partners in our parents' fall" means the sin of Adam and Eve. Yet, because of Christ ("our heavenly Adam") we are made alive (1 Corinthians 15:20-22).

Stanza 7

Ris'n with Him we upward move, Alleluia!

Still we seek the things above, Alleluia!

Still pursue, and kiss the Son, Alleluia!

Seated on His Father's throne, Alleluia!

As in Christ we are risen, we continue to *seek the things above, where Christ is, seated at the right hand of God; set your minds on things above, not on earthly things* (Colossians 3:1-2); and pursue a close relationship with Jesus, the Son, who sits at the right hand of the throne of God the Father (Luke 1:26-33).

Stanza 8

Scarce on earth a thought bestow, Alleluia!

Dead to all we leave below, Alleluia!

Heav'n our aim, and love abode, Alleluia!

Had our life with Christ in God, Alleluia!

As followers of Christ, we are dead to our old self and to the things of this earth. Our aim in life is to spend eternity with Christ in heaven, loving Him, and worshiping God.

Stanza 9

Hid till Christ our life appear, Alleluia!

Glorious in His members here, Alleluia!

Joined to Him, we then shall shine, Alleluia!

All immortal, all divine, Alleluia!

What a wonderful reminder that we are *hidden with Christ in God* (Colossians 3:3). Since we are joined to Christ, and we shine with the light of His salvation, mercy, and love, we live with Him for eternity.

Stanza 10

Hail the Lord of earth and heaven, Alleluia!

Praise to Thee by both be given, Alleluia!

Thee we greet triumphant now, Alleluia!

Hail the Resurrection, thou, Alleluia!

Because Jesus defeated death and arose from the grave, earth and heaven proclaim Him Lord; especially as the

One who triumphed over death and destroyed its power (Hebrews 2:14-15).

Stanza 11

King of glory, Soul of bliss, Alleluia!
Everlasting life is this, Alleluia!
Thee to know, Thy pow'r to prove, Alleluia!
Thus to sing, and thus to love, Alleluia!

The resurrection brings joy that overflows through our praise. Finally, we have arrived in heaven where we are with the King of Glory and have seen the power of God, so we express our love and worship of Him eternally.

✝ Jesus finished the work His Father had sent Him to do—redeem sinners! Have you been redeemed or saved? If so, write a prayer thanking God for redeeming you. If you have not been redeemed or saved, read "Do You Know the Jesus About Whom You Have Been Reading?" on page 235. Also talk with a trusted Christian friend who can help you understand how you can be redeemed (saved) through the finished work of Christ on the cross.

✟ You read that "our aim in life for followers of Christ is to spend eternity with Christ in heaven, loving Him, and worshiping God." Describe how you are preparing to spend eternity with Christ in heaven.

Implications of the Resurrection for Addicts

It is commonly said that the king of fears is the fear of death. If you have experienced the so-called pandemic years of 2020 through early 2022, then you know how paralyzing and terrifying the fear of death can be. People make irrational choices when they are afraid they might die, especially unbelievers, but even believers are afraid to die. And yet the Bible clearly articulates how we should learn to think about the fear of death in Hebrews 2:14-15:

> *14Now since the children have flesh and blood in common, Jesus also shared in these, so that through his death he might destroy the one holding*

the power of death—that is, the devil—¹⁵and free
those who were held in slavery all their lives by the
fear of death.

You no longer have to live enslaved to the fear of death if you are trusting in the One True God, Jesus Christ, who was crucified and raised from death to life.

His resurrection is a foretaste of your resurrection after your death. God is faithful to His promises. He has provided you with a new identity because He has adopted you into His family as His precious child. He does not promise a pain free life without suffering, but He does promise to call you to Himself for eternity when you place your faith and trust in Jesus Christ alone. He has even provided you with everything you need to say "no thanks" to sin and temptation according to 2 Peter 1:3-4:

> *³His divine power has granted to us all things that*
> *pertain to life and godliness, through the*
> *knowledge of him who called us to his own glory*
> *and excellence,⁴ by which he has granted to us his*
> *precious and very great promises, so that through*
> *them you may become partakers of the divine*
> *nature, having escaped from the corruption that is*
> *in the world because of sinful desire.* (ESV)

Belief in your resurrection upon your death requires faith. But it is not a blind faith, it is an informed faith from God's own mouth as the Bible teaches you that you can trust this very promise of God. You may want to rehearse it daily especially if you are prone to fear. In Matthew 10:28, Jesus instructed His disciples specifically about the fear of death: *"Don't fear those who kill the body but are not able to kill the soul; rather, fear him who is able to destroy both soul and body in hell.* Jesus trusted God to resurrect Him. He knew who to fear and who has all of the power to accomplish whatever He wills.

So, in your efforts to maintain sobriety, keep your focus on the command Jesus taught in Matthew 6:33: *But seek first the kingdom of God and his righteousness, and all these things will be provided for you.* Again, it is another reminder that God has given you all that you need, and He knows what you need before you even know what you need! He will continue to be in control of your life and to lead you in the paths in which He wants you to go.

Your responsibility is to not make any provision[81] for your flesh, but to put on thoughts, words, and actions that are biblical and Christlike according to Romans 13:14: *But put*

---

[81] Think or plan in advance to do something.

on the Lord Jesus Christ, and don't make plans to gratify the desires of the flesh, to gratify its desires. Then, you are to obey Galatians 5:16-17: *[16]I say then, walk by the Spirit and you will certainly not carry out the desire of the flesh. [17]For the flesh desires what is against the Spirit, and the Spirit desires what is against the flesh; these are opposed to each other, so that you don't do what you want.*

The Bible never says you will not have temptations or cravings for your drug of choice. The Bible says to put on the righteousness of Christ by walking in the Spirit which must be done in partnership with the Word of God. You must study and then put into practice the Word of God. It is not good enough to read it only, if you do not allow it to change your beliefs and your actions!

Transformation is a two-step process of putting off the flesh and putting on the Holy Spirit. Walking in the Spirit implies that you are moving forward, and it is an action statement that is your responsibility to do. And, when God calls you to do something, He will give you the ability to do it according to the spiritual gifts He gives you, for His good pleasure, and for His own glory.

Celebrate the resurrection of Jesus Christ today because you, too, will be resurrected when your time on earth comes to an end, as it will for all people. But your time here is only the preface and introductory chapter to the rest of your life and the adventures you will have in the next, eternal life to come. That will be the largest part of your life and a book that will never end.

✟ You read that Jesus "provided you with everything you need to say 'no thanks' to sin and temptation." Write down some of the things Jesus has provided that enable you to say "no thanks" to sin and temptation.

✠ You read that in your efforts to maintain sobriety, keep your focus on the command Jesus taught, to *seek first the kingdom of God and his righteousness* …. Describe things you can do to *seek first the kingdom of God and his righteousness.*

Hymn of Response

What is our response to the risen Lord? We *continually offer up to God a sacrifice of praise, that is, the fruit of lips that confess his name* (Hebrews 13:15). Part of our continual sacrifice of praise to God certainly includes hymns which we sing praising Him for saving us. Frances (Fanny) Jane Crosby[82] gives us reasons for praising God and helps us respond to Christ with joyful praise through the lyrics she wrote, *Praise Him! Praise Him!* She based it on Psalm 146:1-2. Chester G. Allen composed the tune *Lazio (Joyful Praise).*[83]

---

[82] See "Who Was Frances (Fanny) Jane Crosby?" on p 200.
[83] See "Who Composed the Tune *Lazio (Joyful Praise)*?" on p 201.

Join us in singing our praises to Jesus, our Redeemer.

Stanza 1

Praise Him! Praise Him! Jesus, our blessed Redeemer!

Sing, O Earth, His wonderful love proclaim!

Hail Him! Hail Him! Highest archangels in glory;

Strength and honor give to His holy Name!

Like a shepherd, Jesus will guard His children,

In His arms He carries them all day long.

Because of His rich mercy and great love for us, Jesus is our blessed Redeemer (Ephesians 2:4-5). We respond by proclaiming His love to everyone. Even the highest archangels in heaven worship Him. We then emphasize another aspect of the character of Jesus, who is also our Shepherd who cares for and carries us.

Refrain

Praise Him! Praise Him! Tell of His excellent greatness;

Praise Him! Praise Him! Ever in joyful song!

As we sing the refrain, we echo Psalm 150.

> [1]*Hallelujah! Praise God in his sanctuary. Praise him in his mighty expanse.* [2]*Praise him for his powerful acts; praise him for his abundant greatness.* [3]*Praise him with trumpet blast; praise*

him with harp and lyre. ⁴Praise him with tambourine and dance; praise him with strings and flute. ⁵Praise him with resounding cymbals; praise him with clashing cymbals. ⁶Let everything that breathes praise the LORD. Hallelujah!

Stanza 2

Praise Him! Praise Him! Jesus, our blessed Redeemer!
For our sins He suffered, and bled, and died.
He our Rock, our hope of eternal salvation,
Hail Him! Hail Him! Jesus the Crucified.
Sound His praises! Jesus who bore our sorrows,
Love unbounded, wonderful, deep and strong.

We praise Jesus who suffered, bled, and died to give us Hope of our eternal salvation. Because He loved us, He bore our sorrows and sins.

Stanza 3

Praise Him! Praise Him! Jesus, our blessed Redeemer!
Heav'nly portals loud with hosannas ring!
Jesus, Savior, reigneth forever and ever;
Crown Him! Crown Him! Prophet, and Priest, and King!
Christ is coming! over the world victorious,
Pow'r and glory unto the Lord belong.

191

Heavenly portals are loud with praises to Jesus whose *kingdom will have no end* (Luke 1:33). When we proclaim, "Crown Him!" we are proclaiming Christ is Prophet, Priest, and King in our hearts right now. We are also waiting and anticipating His coming again!

☩ In this hymn we sing of the reasons we have to praise Jesus. List at least five reasons you have to praise Jesus.

☩ In the third stanza we proclaim Christ is Prophet, Priest, and King in our hearts right now. Describe how to ensure that Christ is Prophet, Priest, and King in your heart?

Prayer

Gracious Heavenly Father, our words are inadequate to thank You for Jesus, our blessed Redeemer. As we read, study, memorize, meditate, and contemplate upon Your Word, help us live in a way that praises and glorifies You. In Jesus' Name, Amen.

Remember that He is Risen, Indeed!

"Through His death and resurrection, your Hope— Jesus—conquered death, sin, external temptations (Matthew 4:1-11), and the devil. God offers the certain promise of Hope in Jesus to everyone! The only pathway to the certainty of Hope comes exclusively through Christ." – Mark Shaw[84]

Prayers, Notes, & Questions

NOTE: If you need more room, see page 239.

---

[84] *Advent: Meditations for Addicts*, Shirley Crowder & Mark Shaw, The Addiction Connection, 2020.

Supplemental Scripture Reading

Isaiah 53:1-12

¹*Who has believed what we have heard? And to whom has the arm of the LORD been revealed?* ²*He grew up before him like a young plant and like a root out of dry ground. He didn't have an impressive form or majesty that we should look at him, no appearance that we should desire him.* ³*He was despised and rejected by men, a man of suffering who knew what sickness was. He was like someone people turned away from; he was despised, and we didn't value him.* ⁴*Yet he himself bore our sicknesses, and he carried our pains; but we in turn regarded him stricken, struck down by God, and afflicted.* ⁵*But he was pierced because of our rebellion, crushed because of our iniquities; punishment for our peace was on him, and we are healed by his wounds.*

⁶*We all went astray like sheep; we all have turned to our own way; and the LORD has punished him for the iniquity of us all.* ⁷*He was oppressed and afflicted, yet he did not open his mouth. Like a lamb led to the slaughter and like a sheep silent before her shearers, he did not open his mouth.* ⁸*He was taken away because of oppression and judgment; and who considered his fate? For he was cut off from the land of the living; he was struck because of my people's rebellion.*

⁸*He was assigned a grave with the wicked, but he was with a rich man at his death, because he had done no violence and had not spoken deceitfully.* ¹⁰*Yet the LORD was pleased to crush him severely. When you make him a guilt offering, he will see his*

seed, he will prolong his days, and by his hand, the LORD's pleasure will be accomplished. ¹¹After his anguish, he will see light and be satisfied. By his knowledge, my righteous servant will justify many, and he will carry their iniquities. ¹²Therefore I will give him the many as a portion, and he will receive the mighty as spoil, because he willingly submitted to death, and was counted among the rebels; yet he bore the sin of many and interceded for the rebels.

Supplemental Scripture Reading

Matthew 28:1-6

¹After the Sabbath, as the first day of the week was dawning, Mary Magdalene and the other Mary went to view the tomb. ²There was a violent earthquake, because an angel of the Lord descended from heaven and approached the tomb. He rolled back the stone and was sitting on it. ³His appearance was like lightning, and his clothing was as white as snow. ⁴The guards were so shaken by fear of him that they became like dead men. ⁵The angel told the women, "Don't be afraid, because I know you are looking for Jesus who was crucified. ⁶"He is not here. For he has risen, just as he said. Come and see the place where he lay.

Supplemental Scripture Reading

Luke 24:1-12

[1]*On the first day of the week, very early in the morning, they came to the tomb, bringing the spices they had prepared.* [2]*They found the stone rolled away from the tomb.* [3]*They went in but did not find the body of the Lord Jesus.* [4]*While they were perplexed about this, suddenly two men stood by them in dazzling clothes.* [5]*So the women were terrified and bowed down to the ground. "Why are you looking for the living among the dead?" asked the man.* [6]*"He is not here, but he has risen! Remember how he spoke to you when he was still in Galilee,* [7]*"saying, 'It is necessary that the Son of Man be betrayed into the hands of sinful men, be crucified, and rise on the third day'?"* [8]*And they remembered his words.*

[9]*Returning from the tomb, they reported all these things to the Eleven and to all the rest.* [10]*Mary Magdalene, Joanna, Mary the mother of James, and the other women with them were telling the apostles these things.* [11]*But these words seemed like nonsense to them, and they did not believe the women.* [12]*Peter, however, got up and ran to the tomb. When he stooped to look in, he saw only the linen cloths. So he went away, amazed at what had happened.*

Who Was Charles Wesley?

Charles Wesley[85] lived from 1701 to 1788. He was the eighteenth child of Susanna and Samuel Wesley. His brother, John Wesley, was also a hymn writer. There are questions about who wrote some hymns, Charles or John.

Charles and John founded a movement that we now know as the Methodist denomination.

Hymn writing came easily to Charles who wrote over six thousand hymns. Many of these hymns are expressions of his feelings on important occasions like his conversion, his marriage, and many scenes of Scripture.

In addition to *Christ the Lord is Risen Today*, he also wrote the beautiful hymn, *Jesus, the Very Thought of Thee*.

---

[85] https://bit.ly/Charles-Wesley

Who Composed the Tune *Easter Hymn*?

We do not know who composed the tune *Easter Hymn*.[86] This tune, to which we now sing *Christ the Lord is Risen Today*, has been altered through the years, as have the lyrics.

In addition to *Easter Hymn* being the tune for Wesley's *Christ the Lord is Risen Today*, it is also the tune for Susan H. Peterson's *Lord, We Come and Offer Praise*, and Friedrich Gottlieb Klopstock's *Lord, Remove the Veil Away*.

---

[86] https://bit.ly/ChristtheLord

Who Was Frances (Fanny) Jane Crosby?

Frances (Fanny) Jane Crosby [87] lived from 1820 to 1915 in New York and Connecticut. When she was six weeks old, she was blinded by the actions of an incompetent doctor. She was the wife of Alexander Van Alstyne, an organist who, like Fanny, was blind. She was one of the most prolific hymn writers in history, writing over eight thousand hymns. Fanny wrote hymns under more than one hundred pseudonyms.

In addition to writing the lyrics for *Praise Him! Praise Him!* she also wrote the lyrics for *Blessed Assurance,* one of her best-known hymns.

---

[87] https://bit.ly/FJCrosby

Who Composed the Tune
Lazio (Joyful Praise)?

Chester G. Allen[88] lived from 1838 to 1878 in New York. He composed the tune *Lazio (Joyful Praise)* to which we sing *Praise Him! Praise Him!* He was a teacher, composer, and music writer. He included many of his own compositions in collections of music for schools and churches.

In addition to writing the tune for *Praise Him! Praise Him!* he also composed the tune for *Christ is Born Today*.

---

[88] https://bit.ly/CGAllen

Go Tell

Begin the Sunday After Easter

Celebrate Easter This Week

Begin each day by confessing your sin and asking God to forgive your sin.

Pray your heart will be open to the correction, encouragement, and teaching of God's Word.

Pray the Lord will ignite your passion to know Him better and enable you to go tell the Good News to all those whom He brings across your path.

Take your time as you work through each day's reading to consider prayerfully and write out your answers to the exercises.

Day 1

Old Testament Prophecy

[1]The LORD said to Abram: Go out from your land, your relatives, and your father's house to the land that I will show you. [2]I will make you into a great nation, I will bless you, I will make your name great, and you will be a blessing. [3]I will bless those who bless you, I will curse anyone who treats you with contempt, and all the peoples on earth will be blessed through you (Genesis 12:1-3).

⁵*This is what God, the* LORD, *says —who created the heavens and stretched them out, who spread out the earth and what comes from it, who gives breath to the people on it and spirit to those who walk on it —*⁶*I am the* LORD. *I have called you for a righteous purpose, and I will hold you by your hand. I will watch over you, and I will appoint you to be a covenant for the people and a light to the nations,* ⁷*in order to open blind eyes, to bring out prisoners from the dungeon, and those sitting in darkness from the prison house.* ⁸*I am the* LORD. *That is my name, and I will not give my glory to another or my praise to idols.* ⁹*The past events have indeed happened. Now I declare new events; I announce them to you before they occur"* (Isaiah 42:5-9).

✝ In the Isaiah passage we read, *I am the* LORD. *That is my name, and I will not give my glory to another or my praise to idols.* An idol is any person, place, or thing that we place in a higher position in our lives than God. List one or two idols you are now placing, or that you have in the past placed, in a higher position than God.

New Testament Fulfillment

8Now the Scripture saw in advance that God would justify the Gentiles by faith and proclaimed the gospel ahead of time to Abraham, saying, **All the nations will be blessed through you.** *9Consequently those who have faith are blessed with Abraham, who had faith* (Galatians 3:8-9).

8When he took the scroll, the four living creatures and the twenty-four elders fell down before the Lamb. Each one had a harp and golden bowls filled with incense, which are the prayers of the saints. 9And they sang a new song: You are worthy to take the scroll and to open its seals, because you were slaughtered, and you purchased people for God by your blood from every tribe and language and people and nation. 10You made them a kingdom and priests to our God, and they will reign on the earth. (Revelation 5:8-10).

✞ In the Galatians passage we read God *proclaimed the gospel ahead of time to Abraham* so that through him **All the nations will be blessed.** In what ways have you been blessed by someone whom God prepared in advance to bless you?

Symbol of Easter

Turn back to the chapter title page (p 203) and look at the illustration that represents taking the Word of God—the Good News—to everyone everywhere. If that sounds familiar to you, perhaps you have heard of The Great Commission.

Before we take a careful look at The Great Commission, we will take a step back and make sure we know what a "commission" is. "Commission" means a person is given "the authority to act for, in behalf of, or in place of another."[89]

Look at what Matthew recorded about Christ's final words to His disciples after His death and resurrection, and just before He ascended into heaven. Matthew 28:16-20[90] is the passage that we most often hear referred to as The Great Commission.

---

[89] www.Merriam-Webster.com/dictionary
[90] See "Supplemental Scripture Reading: The Great Commission" on p 228.

16The eleven disciples traveled to Galilee, to the mountain where Jesus had directed them. 17When they saw him, they worshiped, but some doubted.

18Jesus came near and said to them, "All authority has been given to me in heaven and on earth.

19Go, therefore, and make disciples of all nations, baptizing them in the name of the Father and of the Son and of the Holy Spirit, 20teaching them to observe everything I have commanded you. And remember, I am with you always, to the end of the age."

It may surprise some of you that we are going to look in the Old Testament as we seek a deeper understanding of The Great Commission. Passages in the Old Testament build the foundation for the The Great Commission we find in the New Testament.

Turn back to the Day 1 Old Testament Prophecy (p 204). If you are not familiar with biblical history and the life of Abraham, you may be confused as to why we have chosen Genesis 12:1-3 for our Old Testament Prophecy. As we look at God's promise to Abraham, we see that God was also giving Abraham the commission to bless all the nations. Through Abraham and his descendants, the world would witness God's salvation so that all people in all the nations would have the opportunity to come to know Him and His blessings through their saving knowledge of God.

In the Isaiah 42:5-9 prophecy, God promises to stand by and strengthen the Messiah who came *to open blind eyes, to bring out prisoners from the dungeon, and those sitting in darkness from the prison house.*

The Day 1 New Testament Fulfillment (p 206) tells us that God fulfilled the promise He made to Abraham.

> *⁸Now the Scripture saw in advance that God would justify the Gentiles by faith and proclaimed the gospel ahead of time to Abraham, saying,* **All the nations will be blessed through you.** *⁹Consequently those who have faith are blessed with Abraham, who had faith* (Galatians 3:8-9).

Now that we see God's plan to take the Good News to all nations, we will look at The Great Commission.

A great thing about God is that He did not just give us a command, "make disciple-makers" and then leave it up to us to figure out how to accomplish making disciple-makers. We do not go out because we have the idea to go. Jesus gave us the authority to go. He also gave us His

Word which the Holy Spirit uses to teach us, thus enabling us to be obedient to His command. In addition, remember that God does not call us to do something that He has not already prepared and equipped us with His enabling power to accomplish.

Since we as Christ-followers have been saved, we have an enormous responsibility to go tell the Good News. The goal for us as we proclaim this Good News is to live a life that shows the watching world that we are Christ-followers walking in His empowering authority, enablement, mercy, grace, and kindness.

The Great Commission certainly includes the imperative to evangelize our family, community, city, state, and the world and it means so much more! In this Commission, Jesus was also saying that as you go about doing the things God has called you to do, in the places He has called you to do them, make disciple-makers.

Do you see the difference? As you go about being a student, mom, physician, electrician, dad, teacher, or homemaker, make disciple-makers. This means to teach other Christ-followers the Word of God and how to apply this Word in their day-to-day lives. We are to share with others what we know about God. It does not have to be in a formal classroom setting. It can be while we are cooking, teaching, or exercising. Making disciple-makers is a way of life for Christ-followers. We are to disciple others, who will in turn disciple others, who will in turn disciple others, and so on. We are to make disciple-makers.

To be faithful disciple-makers we start at home and go out from there to our church, work, community, city, state, nation, and the world.

About now some of you may be thinking, "I can't go to Africa or even to Utah!" You may not be able to go, but you can pray for, encourage, and financially support those who can go.

Remember that when Jesus told us to make disciples of all nations, He was talking about making disciples of all the people from all the nations, as we see when we refer to the Day 1 New Testament Fulfillment passage (p 206). We see the creatures and elders falling down before the Lamb (God).

> *And they sang a new song: You are worthy to take the scroll and to open its seals, because you were slaughtered, and you purchased people for God by your blood from every tribe and language and people and nation* (Revelation 5:9).

✝ We read in the Isaiah 42:5-9 prophecy, God promised to stand by and strengthen the Messiah who came *to open blind eyes, to bring out prisoners from the dungeon, and those sitting in darkness from the prison house.* Describe how Jesus has opened your blind eyes, brought you out from the dungeon, and from sitting in darkness in the prison house.

✝ The goal as we proclaim this Good News is to live a life that shows the watching world that we are Christ-followers walking in His empowering authority, enablement, mercy, grace, and kindness. Describe how you can show the world that you are a Christ-follower. If you are not a Christ-follower, read "Do You Know the Jesus About Whom You Have Been Reading?" on page 235. Also talk with a trusted Christian friend who can help you understand how to come to a saving knowledge of Jesus.

Hymn of Easter

O Zion Haste is possibly one of the best mission hymns that communicates the responsibility of the church (the people) to carry out The Great Commission. Mary Ann Faulkner Thomson[91] wrote the lyrics and James Walch composed the tune, *Tidings,*[92] to which we sing it.

In addition to being based on Matthew 28:16-20, it is also based on Isaiah 52:7:

> *How beautiful on the mountains are the feet of the herald, who proclaims peace, who brings new of good things, who proclaims salvation, who says to Zion, "Your God reigns!"*

Stanza 1

O Zion, haste, thy mission high fulfilling,

To tell to all the world that God is light,

That He who made all nations is not willing

One soul should perish, lost in shades of night.

---

[91] See "Who Was Mary Ann Faulkner Thomson?" on p 232.
[92] See "Who Composed the Tune *Tidings*?" on p 233.

Zion represents the church—the people of God. This stanza urges us to continue our mission—sharing the Good News—with a sense of urgency. We are to go tell everyone that "God is light." We also are reminded that *the Lord does not delay his promise, as some understand delay but is patient with you, not wanting any to perish but all to come to repentance* (2 Peter 3:9).

Refrain

Publish glad tidings, tidings of peace;

Tidings of Jesus, redemption and release.

We are to go tell the message of Christ to every person in the world, including those struggling with an addiction. This is a message of His peace, our redemption and release from the bondage of sin.

Stanza 2

Behold how many thousands still are lying

Bound in the darksome prison house of sin,

With none to tell them of the Savior's dying,

Or of the life He died for them to win.

Here we recognize that there are so many people all over the world who are still "bound in the darksome prison house of sin" and there is no one to tell them how Christ *humbled himself by becoming obedient to the point of death*—

even to death on a cross (Philippians 2:8) to take upon Himself their sin and the punishment they deserve. We also want to make sure they hear that Christ died so they, and we, can have abundant life now and for eternity (John 10:10).

Stanza 3

Proclaim to every people, tongue, and nation
That God, in whom they live and move, is love;
Tell how He stooped to save His lost creation,
And died on earth that we might live above.

Again, we are proclaiming the Good News to everyone everywhere. The God we proclaim is the very God in whom *we live and move and have our being* (Acts 17:24-28). We want to be certain everyone knows that the God of love left heaven and came down to earth as Jesus. He lived as fully God and fully man so that He could atone for our sin, enabling us to live victorious lives here on earth, and to live eternally with Him in heaven.

Stanza 4

'Tis thine to save from peril of perdition
The souls for whom the Lord His life laid down:
Beware lest, slothful to fulfill thy mission,
Thou lose one jewel that should deck His crown.

Because Jesus atoned for our sin, it is our responsibility to share the truth of God's Word so that people will be saved. We are not to be lazy in fulfilling our mission (commission). It is an honor to go tell the Good News of Jesus.

Stanza 5

Give of thy sons to bear the message glorious;
Give of thy wealth to speed them on their way;
Pour out thy soul for them in prayer victorious;
O Zion, haste to bring the brighter day.

Here we are reminding ourselves and those who are singing with us that we can be part of going and making disciple-makers, baptizing them, and teaching them to observe (obey) God's commands. We can send our children and others to share the Good News with everyone. We can also support them with our money and other resources to help them in their missions. We are reminding ourselves to pray earnestly that those who hear the Good News will come to a saving knowledge of Jesus Christ.

Stanza 6

He comes again! O Zion, ere thou meet Him,
Make known to every heart His saving grace:

Let none whom he Hath ransomed fail to greet Him,

Through thy neglect, unfit to see His face.

Since Jesus Christ is coming again, we must prepare for His coming by making certain that everyone everywhere knows they can be saved by grace through faith in Him (Ephesians 2:3-10). We are to be ready to greet Him when He returns!

✝ The second stanza tells us that there are many people all over the world who are still "bound in the darksome prison house of sin" without anyone to tell them that Christ atoned and took the punishment they deserved for their sin. Describe how you were "bound in the darksome prison house of sin" before you were saved. If you are not saved, read "Do You Know the Jesus About Whom You Have Been Reading?" on page 235. Also talk with a trusted Christian friend who can help you understand how to get freed from the darksome prison house of sin.

✝ What are some ways you can participate in sharing the gospel with everyone everywhere?

Implications of Go Tell for Addicts

Until your life has ended, and you are called home to heaven, you have an opportunity to love God by loving His children and reaching the lost with the Hope of the Gospel. Your life is but a vapor (James 4:14). This biblical truth is meant to compel you to urgency. You may have lost friends who are or are not addicted. Regardless, you are the messenger called to go and make disciples by proclaiming the excellencies of Christ in the Good News of the Gospel.

You may reach people who are uniquely yours to reach. You will not lead anyone to salvation with a worldly message that addiction is a disease, but you will with a message that the heart desires fueling addictive choices are sin. And you have a remedy for sin in that they can repent and place their faith in Jesus Christ alone for the forgiveness and remission of their sins. This message is the Gospel. It truly is good news that is not often thought to apply to addiction, though it most certainly does.

Of course, when you want to reach out to a still-addicted friend, do not do so alone. That would be unwise and create unnecessary temptation for you. Reach out with a trusted Christian friend and a strong believer. Remember that you are just one beggar showing an unsaved beggar where to find the Bread of Life. God revealed the truth to you first, so your job is to tell everyone you know about Jesus Christ, the Bread of Life.

It is a great honor and privilege to serve God in this way. He delights to use you for His own glory. To share in this endeavor is a wonderful blessing to you and to those whom you might lead away from hell and the impending wrath of God. You will need to live each day as though it is your last. You will need to keep your eyes on eternity, as Colossians 3:1-4 says:

> *[1]So if you have been raised with Christ, seek the things above, where Christ is, seated at the right hand of God. [2]Set your minds on things above, not on earthly things. [3]For you died, and your life is*

219

hidden with Christ in God. ⁴When Christ, who is your life, appears, then you also will appear with him in glory.

God saved you for His purposes. Discover the exciting adventure He has in store for you when you simply live each day to do His will!

✞ You read that "when you want to reach out to a still-addicted friend, do not do so alone. That would be unwise and create unnecessary temptation for you." Describe at least two ways reaching out to a still-addicted friend alone would be unwise and create unnecessary temptation.

✞ You read that "to share in this endeavor of reaching out to a still-addicted friend is a wonderful blessing to you and to those you might lead away from hell and the impending wrath of God. You will need to live each day as though it is your last. You will need to keep your eyes on eternity." Explain what changes you need to make in order to live each day as though it is your last day here on earth.

DAY 5

Hymn of Response

How are we to respond to The Great Commission? We are to be cognizant that we have a story to tell all the nations. Henry Ernest Nichol[93] wrote the lyrics and tune for the wonderful missionary hymn, *We've a Story to Tell to the Nations.*

This hymn helps motivate and inspire Christ-followers to go tell the Good News to everyone everywhere.

Its dynamic, energetic tune gives us a sense of going out enthusiastically with unswerving determination to tell the Good News to all those with whom we come in contact.

Join us in singing triumphantly, as we proclaim.

---

[93] See "Who Was Henry Ernest Nichol?" on p 234.

Stanza 1

We've a story to tell to the nations,

That shall turn their hearts to the right,

A story of truth and mercy,

A story of peace and light,

A story of peace and light.

The Good News is the story all Christ-followers can tell because we have experienced the life-changing transformation of a relationship with Jesus Christ. The purpose of this story that we are to tell is to turn the hearts of the sinful people of every nation to God. This is a story of the truth of God as we see in John 8:32-36:

> [32]*"You will know the truth, and the truth will set you free.* [33]*We are descendants of Abraham," they answered him, "and we have never been enslaved to anyone. How can you say, 'You will become free'?"* [34]*Jesus responded, "Truly I tell you, everyone who commits sin is a slave of sin.* [35]*A slave does not remain in the household forever, but a son does remain forever.* [36]*So if the Son sets you free, you really will be free.*

It is also a story of peace that can only come because *God was pleased to have all his fullness dwell in him, and through him to reconcile everything to himself, whether things on earth or things in heaven, by making peace through his blood, shed on the cross* (Colossians 1:19-20).

Refrain
For the darkness shall turn to dawning,
And the dawning to noonday bright;
And Christ's great kingdom
Shall come on earth,
The kingdom of love and light.

When the Kingdom of God comes to earth, the Light of the World, Jesus, forgives our sins and saves us. The darkness of our sin, including addiction, turns from darkness to early morning's light, which turns into the brightness of a relationship with Christ. This is a kingdom of love and life. Our salvation comes only through Jesus Christ.

Stanza 2
We've a song to be sung to the nations,
That shall lift their hearts to the Lord,
A song that shall conquer evil
And shatter the spear and sword,
And shatter the spear and sword.

Christ-followers have a song to sing to everyone everywhere. This song will lift the weary and heavy-laden hearts of the hearers to the Lord so that they may come to Him for rest (Matthew 11:28-30).

This song shall conquer evil and shatter our weapons of war because *we do not wage war according to the flesh, since the weapons of warfare are not of the flesh, ⁴but are powerful through God for the demolition of strongholds. We demolish arguments ⁴and every proud thing that is raised up against the knowledge of God, and we take every thought captive to obey Christ* (2 Corinthians 10:3-5).

Stanza 3

We've a message to give to the nations,

That the Lord who reigns up above

Has sent us His Son to save us,

And show us that God is love,

And show us that God is love.

Christ-followers have a message to tell all the people of all the nations. The message comes from our Father in heaven, and it tells how He sent His Son, Jesus, to be our Savior (Luke 2:11) and to save us through His shed blood. In this message we see that *God loved the world in this way.*

He gave his one and only Son, so that everyone who believes in him will not perish but have eternal life (John 3:16).

Stanza 4

We've a Savior to show to the nations,
Who the path of sorrow has trod,
That all of the world's great peoples
Might come to the truth of God,
Might come to the truth of God.

As we continue telling the story, singing the song, and delivering the message, we show our Savior to everyone everywhere so that they have the opportunity to "come to the truth of God." Our fully God, Jesus became fully man and walked the "path of sorrow" to bring us salvation that enables us to live victorious lives here on earth and to praise Him for all eternity.

Jesus walked this path because *the Son of Man* [came] *to seek and to save the lost* (Luke 19:10) in order to reconcile us to God (2 Corinthians 5:17-19).

✟ John 8:32 and 36 says *you will know the truth, and the truth will set you free … So if the Son sets you free, you really will be free.* Describe how the truth sets you free from your sin.

✟ In the fourth stanza, we sing that we have "a Savior to show to the nations." In what ways can we show the Savior to the nations.

Prayer

Gracious Heavenly Father, forgive me for not being obedient to share the gospel with those whom You place in my path. Enable me to move forward without hesitation when You call me to share the gospel and to proclaim boldly the gospel message through everything I say and do. In Jesus' Name, Amen.

Remember to Go Tell

"Whatever we do, we must not treat The Great Commission like it's the Great Suggestion." – Charles R. Swindoll

Prayers, Notes, & Questions

NOTE: If you need more room, see page 239.

Supplemental Scripture Reading

The Great Commission

As we delve in a little deeper, we also consider that because the Bible was written by many different people who were inspired by the Holy Spirit of God, the accounts we read of various events are often presented a little differently since each writer's perspective is different. The Gospels—Matthew, Mark, Luke, and John—are good examples of this difference.

Look at what the Gospels tell us about Christ's final words to His disciples after His death and resurrection, just before He ascended into heaven to sit at the right hand of God Almighty. As Christ-followers today, we are to follow Christ's Commission also.

Do you remember Matthew 28:16-20?

> *16The eleven disciples traveled to Galilee, to the mountain where Jesus had directed them. 17When they saw him, they worshiped, but some doubted. 18Jesus came near and said to them, "All authority has been given to me in heaven and on earth. 19"Go, therefore, and make disciples of all nations, baptizing them in the name of the Father and of the*

Son and of the Holy Spirit, ²⁰*teaching them to observe everything I have commanded you. And remember, I am with you always, to the end of the age."*

Recorded in Mark 16:14-16 we see a little different perspective of Jesus giving The Great Commission.

> ¹⁴*Later he appeared to the Eleven themselves as they were reclining at the table. He rebuked their unbelief and hardness of heart, because they did not believe those who saw him after he had risen. ¹⁵Then he said to them, "Go into all the world and preach the gospel to all creation. ¹⁶Whoever believes and is baptized will be saved, but whoever does not believe will be condemned.*

Recorded in Luke 24:44-49, we see Dr. Luke's perspective.

> ⁴⁴*He told them, "These are my words that I spoke to you while I was still with you — that everything written about me in the Law of Moses, the Prophets, and the Psalms must be fulfilled." ⁴⁵Then he opened their minds to understand the Scriptures. ⁴⁶He also said to them, "This is what is written: The Messiah would suffer and rise from the dead the third day, ⁴⁷and repentance for*

229

forgiveness of sins would be proclaimed in his name to all the nations, beginning at Jerusalem. [48]You are witnesses of these things. [49]And look, I am sending you what my Father promised. As for you, stay in the city until you are empowered from on high."

Recorded in John 20:19-22 we see yet another perspective.

[19]When it was evening of that first day of the week, the disciples were gathered together with the doors locked because they feared the Jews. Jesus came, stood among them, and said to them, "Peace be with you."

[20]Having said this, he showed them his hands and his side. So the disciples rejoiced when they saw the Lord. [21]Jesus said to them again, "Peace to you. As the Father has sent me, I also send you." [22]After saying this, he breathed on them and said, "Receive the Holy Spirit."

Dr. Luke also wrote the book of Acts that tells how the disciples were obedient to The Great Commission. In Acts 1:8, Luke gives us a little more detail than he recorded in the Luke 24 passage.

"But you will receive power when the Holy Spirit has come on you, and you will be my witnesses in Jerusalem, in all Judea and Samaria, and to the end of the earth."

Who Was Mary Ann Faulkner Thomson?

Mary Ann Faulkner Thomson[94] (sometimes listed as Thompson) lived from 1834 to 1923. Born in London, England, she was the wife of John Thomson, Philadelphia Free Library's first librarian. They emigrated to the United States from England in 1881. She died in Philadelphia, Pennsylvania. Five of her twelve children died in infancy.

It appears that *O Zion Haste* was the only hymn Mrs. Thomson wrote.

---

[94] https://bit.ly/MAFThomson

Who Composed the Tune *Tidings*?

James Walch[95] lived from 1837 to 1901 in England and Wales. He served as organist at several different churches in England.

He conducted the Bolton Philharmonic Symphony before moving to Barrow-in-Furness to operate a music business.

In addition to writing the tune, *Tidings*, he also composed the tune, *Eagley*, to which we sing Edward Denny's *Light of the Lonely Pilgrims*.

---

[95] https://bit.ly/JamesWalch

Who Was Henry Ernest Nichol?

Henry Ernest Nichol[96] lived from 1862 to 1926 in Yorkshire, England. Some sources credit Colin Sterne as the lyric writer and tune composer of *We've a Story to Tell*. Sterne is a pseudonym Nichol used. It is a rearrangement of the letters in his middle name, Ernest.

Nichol entered Oxford University with the intent of becoming an engineer but switched to studying music. Many of the hymns he wrote were written specifically for Sunday School anniversaries.

In addition to *We've a Story to Tell to the Nations*, he also wrote numerous hymns and several tunes, including the tune *Kirk Ella*, to which we sing Charles Wesley's hymn, *Angels Speak, Let Man Give Ear*.

---

[96] https://bit.ly/HENichol

Do You Know the Jesus About Whom You Have Been Reading?

If you realize that you do not have a relationship with Jesus—you are unsaved—take a few minutes to read and think through the following so you are prepared for the day you will meet Him face-to-face.

If you are not absolutely certain that you know Him, please do not wait. Pray, using the following to guide you as you think through the following Scriptures.

Everyone has sinned against Holy God and has been separated from Him. *For all have sinned and fall short of the glory of God* (Romans 3:23).

The cost we pay for our sin is eternal death. *For the wages of sin is death, but the gift of God is eternal life in Christ Jesus our Lord* (Romans 6:23).

Even though we were living in our sin, Jesus Christ—the Savior and Lord—loved you and gave His life to take the punishment you deserved to receive for your sin. *Jesus told him, "I am the way, the truth, and the life. No one comes to the Father except through me"* (John 14:6).

For those who know Jesus Christ as Savior, *there is now no condemnation for those in Christ Jesus* (Romans 8:1).

Confess (tell Him) that you have sinned against Him, repent and ask Him to forgive you. *If we confess our sins, he is faithful and righteous to forgive us our sins and to cleanse us from all unrighteousness* (1 John 1:9). Acts 3:19 tells us to *repent and turn back, so that our sins may be wiped out.*

Pray in this way: "Lord, I confess that I am a sinner because I have broken Your law and I am asking you to save me from the just punishment for my sins through Jesus Christ. I repent and place my faith in Christ alone for eternal life."

If you asked Jesus Christ to save you, would you please seek out a trusted Christian friend to share that you are now a Christ-follower so that you can join a community of believers in a local church? Ask them to help you learn more about Jesus and how to serve Him.

The joy of being a Christ-follower is that you may now live in the freedom of God's forgiveness and walk *as God's chosen ones, holy and dearly loved, put on compassion, kindness, humility, gentleness, and patience, bearing with one another and forgiving one another if anyone has a grievance against another. Just as the Lord has forgiven you, so you are also to forgive* (Colossians 3:12-13).

If you have more questions about the topic of asking Jesus Christ to save you, would you please seek out a trusted Christian friend to share those questions with them? Ask them to help you learn more about Jesus and how to serve Him.

You may also contact The Addiction Connection if you need to speak with someone about your relationship with Christ.

Contact us at: info@theaddictionconnection.org

PRAYERS, NOTES, & QUESTIONS (more space)

PRAYERS, NOTES, & QUESTIONS (more space)

PRAYERS, NOTES, & QUESTIONS (more space)

Meet Mark and Shirley

Mark E. Shaw

Mark E. Shaw, DMin, serves as Director of Counseling at Grace Fellowship Church in the Cincinnati / northern Kentucky area. As the Founder of The Addiction Connection, a national network of servant leaders in addictions biblical counseling, Mark is passionate about stirring up local church excitement for the "Hope of the Gospel for the heart of addiction," and seeks to fulfill Ephesians 4:11-16 by equipping the whole church for the work ahead. Mark and his wife Mary have four grown children. The whole family ministers together in various aspects of The Addiction Connection. Dr. Shaw is a graduate of Birmingham Theological Seminary with a Doctor of Ministry in Biblical Counseling, and he maintains ACBC certification as well as a state addictions counselor certification, CADAC II.

Shirley Crowder

Shirley Crowder is passionate about disciple-making, which is conducted in and through a myriad of ministry opportunities including biblical counseling, teaching Bible studies, writing, and music. She serves as Vice President of The Addiction Connection.

Shirley is an award-winning author with several of her articles appearing in "Paper Pulpit" in the Faith section of *The Gadsden* (Alabama) *Times*. She also has published articles for David C. Cook, Student Life, and Woman's Missionary Union publications. She contributes to several blogs and she is published as an author, co-author, and contributing author of twelve books.

Follow the Authors

Follow Mark at:

www.TheAddictionConnection.org
amazon.com/author/markeshaw
https://www.facebook.com/
TheAddictionConnectionTAC/
twitter.com/HisTruthInLove

Follow Shirley at:

www.ThroughtheLensofScripture.org
amazon.com/author/shirleycrowder
www.facebook.com/shirleycrowder
twitter.com/ShirleyJCrowder

Also by the Authors

Mark E. Shaw

ADVENT: Meditations for Addicts – Shirley Crowder & Mark E. Shaw

Addiction-Proof Parenting: Biblical Prevention Strategies – Mark E. Shaw

Cross Talking: A Daily Gospel for Transforming Addicts – Mark E. Shaw

Divine Intervention: Hope & Help for Families of Addicts – Mark E. Shaw

Eating Disorders: Hope for Hungering Souls – Mark E. Shaw, Rachel Bailey, & Bethany Spence

Hope & Help for Chronic Illness – Mark Shaw & Allison Griffin

Hope & Help for Gambling – Mark Shaw

Hope & Help for Marriage – Mark Shaw

Hope & Help for Men as Husbands & Fathers – Mark Shaw

Hope & Help for Self-Injurers & Cutters – Mark Shaw

Hope & Help for Sexual Temptation – Mark Shaw

Hope & Help for Video Game, TV & Internet "Addiction" – Mark Shaw

Hope & Help Through Biblical Counseling – Mark Shaw

How Not to Raise an Addict: Biblical Prevention Strategies – Mark E. Shaw

Paul the Counselor: Counseling and Disciple-Making Modeled by the Apostle – edited by Mark Shaw & Bill Hines

Relapse: Biblical Prevention Strategies – Mark Shaw

Strength in Numbers: The Team Approach to Biblical Counseling – Mark E. Shaw

The Heart of Addiction: A Biblical Perspective – Mark E. Shaw

The Heart of Addiction Leader's Guide – Mark & Mary Shaw

The Heart of Addiction Workbook – Mark E. Shaw

The Pursuit of Perfection: A Biblical Perspective – Mark Shaw & Bill Hines

Understanding Temptation: The War Within Your Heart – Mark E. Shaw

Available at Focus Publishing

(www.FocusPublishing.com)

and at Amazon.com

Shirley Crowder

ADVENT: Meditations for Addicts – Shirley Crowder & Mark E. Shaw

Day by Day: 40 Devotionals for Writers & Creative Types – contributed two devotionals

Glimpses of God: a winter devotional for women – Harriet E. Michael & Shirley Crowder

Glimpses of God: a spring devotional for women – Harriet E. Michael & Shirley Crowder

Glimpses of God: a summer devotional for women – Shirley Crowder & Harriet E. Michael

Glimpses of God: an autumn devotional for women – Shirley Crowder & Harriet E. Michael

Glimpses of Prayer – Shirley Crowder & Harriet E. Michael

Glimpses of the Savior: 50 Meditations for Thanksgiving, Christmas, and the New Year – Shirley Crowder & Harriet E. Michael

Hope for New Beginnings: 31 Devotions for the Adventure – Dr. Howard Eyrich & Shirley Crowder

Paul the Counselor: Counseling and Disciple-Making Modeled by the Apostle – co-wrote Chapter 11: Paul and Women in Ministry

Prayer Warrior Confessions – Harriet E. Michael & Shirley Crowder

Study Guide on Prayer—A Companion to Prayer: It's Not About You – Shirley Crowder

Available on Amazon.com

About the Publisher
The Addiction Connection

The Addiction Connection (TAC) is a collective of biblical counselors and ministries united for the purpose of training and equipping the body of Christ in biblically helping those struggling or suffering with an addiction and their loved ones. A key foundational principle is that an individual, program, and church in our network must embrace the sufficiency of Scripture for dealing with the life-dominating sin issue of idolatrous addictions.

The Addiction Connection helps the local body of Christ reclaim a genuinely biblical approach to ministry to those struggling with addictions through three focal areas: Training, Commissioning, and Resource Networking.

Training

Training is essential to becoming a skilled biblical counselor, especially in the area of life-dominating sins such as addiction. God gives grace as we grow and He wants us to be skilled at handling His Word of truth according to 2 Timothy 2:15: *Be diligent to present yourself to God as one approved, a worker who doesn't need to be ashamed, correctly teaching the word of truth.* Our trainers and supervisors want you to be equipped to do ministry as you seek to see lives transformed by truth and grace (John 1:14).

Commissioning

One of the main things we do at TAC is commission those who are called by God to provide biblical counseling for people struggling with addiction. Commissioned individuals are then listed on our website and available to encourage one another through relational connections. Our commissioning process is more than just taking some training courses. While sound theology is the foundation, our 100% virtual commissioning process is relational and practical: preparing and strengthening you for real ministry to those enslaved to addiction.

Resource Networking

Explore the people, programs, and publications we can confidently recommend to you because each one is committed to God's Word as they offer, "The Hope of the Gospel for the Heart of Addiction."

Chapter Title Page Illustration Credits

Full God and Fully Man

Manger with Shadow of the Cross   p 19
https://www.canstockphoto.com/ginosphotos/

The Triumphal Entry

Donkey and Palm Leaves   p 45
Choat/DepositPhotos.com

The Lord's Supper

Cup and Bread   p 79
MKucova/DepositPhotos.com

I Don't Know the Man!

Peter Denies Christ   p 109
Frank Zimmerman on flickr.com

The Beautiful Cross

The Cross   p 137
WEGPhoto/DepositPhotos.com

He is Risen, Indeed!

Empty Tomb   p 167
RFPhoto/DepositPhotos.com

Go Tell

Bible with World Map   p 203
https://www.canstockphoto.com/georgemuresan/

Quote Index

Hymn Index

Supplemental Scripture Reading Index

Scripture Index

Old Testament Scriptures

New Testament Scriptures

The Addiction Connection
9379 Gunpowder Road
Florence, KY 41042
www.theaddictionconnection.org

Made in United States
North Haven, CT
23 March 2022

17461617R10143